Praise for Tatiana L.

"Dr. Lysenko was one of my Ukrainian teachers in the spring and summer of 2000 as I prepared to become the next American ambassador to Ukraine. She is an excellent teacher who makes every possible effort to help her student learn effectively and to understand the culture which underlies the Ukrainian language... In her publications Dr. Lysenko made a point of introducing different aspects of Ukrainian history and popular culture. By offering these materials and explaining their significance, Dr. Lysenko helped me develop a better intuitive feel for customs and practices that are important to the Ukrainian people... Her new book "The Price of Freedom" is a vital work for university and college libraries, academics and individuals..."

Ambassador Carlos Pascual.

"An excellent book for both reference and entertaining... A truly sumptuous, clearly written... I recommend it to anyone who wants to know more about Ukraine and its people. Ukraine has been a mystery and terra incognita (Latin: unknown land) for many in the Western World since it emerged from shadow of the Soviet Union in 1991. The author presents unique information about ethno-genesis of the Ukrainians, their traditions, ethnic culture and spirituality... Thank you, Tatiana, for writing such an inspiring book."

Professor Ludmila Guslistova,
The George Washington University.

"I love this splendid new book about real Ukrainians and their origin culture. I love the image of Author's mother, beautiful Ukrainian woman and her traditional ethnic costume on the front cover of the book. I am proud of Ukraine and its people. This book is relevant today because it pertains to the events that the whole world is now watching. It pertains to the Revolution of Dignity that is taking place in Kyiv on Independence Square – the Maidan. The invigorating story of the author's life, told in her own words, is connected precisely to what is now taking place in Ukraine. Her book represents the pain of millions of Ukrainians who suffered under the totalitarian regime in Ukraine. This book should be read by the whole world! Glory to Ukraine!

Svitlana Panchenko,
Head of the World Association of Ukrainian Women, London, Great Britain.

"Dr. Lysenko is a talented woman who has accumulated a wealth of experience in her lifetime. She has distinguished herself as a scholar, educator, journalist and writer. Growing up, working and living in a multilingual environment, Tatiana has had the benefit of understanding diversity and through her travel and work in Ukraine and the United States she has acquired a global perspective and appreciation of different cultures and the cross-cultural dimension. Her merits are noted in "Who is Who in Ukraine (Gold Book of Ukraine)" and "Prominent Women of Ukraine (Woman Face of Ukraine)"."

Vera Andrushkiv,
Vice-President of the US-Ukraine Foundation, Washington DC.

THE PRICE *of* FREEDOM

Tatiana Lysenko

Copyright © 2014 Tetyana Lysenko.

All rights reserved. No part of this book may be reproduced, stored, or transmitted by any means—whether auditory, graphic, mechanical, or electronic—without written permission of both publisher and author, except in the case of brief excerpts used in critical articles and reviews. Unauthorized reproduction of any part of this work is illegal and is punishable by law.

ISBN: 978-1-4834-0575-9 (sc)
ISBN: 978-1-4834-0574-2 (e)

Library of Congress Control Number: 2013956471

Because of the dynamic nature of the Internet, any web addresses or links contained in this book may have changed since publication and may no longer be valid. The views expressed in this work are solely those of the author and do not necessarily reflect the views of the publisher, and the publisher hereby disclaims any responsibility for them.

Any people depicted in stock imagery provided by Thinkstock are models, and such images are being used for illustrative purposes only.
Certain stock imagery © Thinkstock.

Lulu Publishing Services rev. date: 1/23/2014

In Memory of My Mother, Maria

Preface

Destiny is not a matter of chance – it is a matter of choice. It is not a thing to be waited for – it is a thing to be achieved.
William Jennings Bryan

With love, I dedicate this book to the immigrants from different part of our beautiful planet Earth, who had found new life in their new chosen Homeland – the land of Liberty – United States of America.

For hundreds of years, immigrants have been coming to America to gain greater freedom and to realize the human dreams, and I am one of them.

I would like to share the story of my life, to tell a true story about the country where I was born. This book is a real-life story; however it is a work of fiction. References to real people, events, organizations, or locales are intended only to provide a sense of authenticity, and are used fictitiously.

Living in this world, people have always asked a multitude of questions: How can we understand the world in which we find ourselves? What is the nature of our reality? Why we have so far different reality? What does it mean for us – to gain freedom in this vast world that is by turns kind and cruel…? In my book I try to give the answers to these questions.

I would like to thank all people, who have been at my side all these years, helping me in getting political asylum in the United States.

Thank you, my dear mother, without you this may never happened. I always remember how you teach me, your brilliant words: "Live in order that your joy, your success, your talent and your knowledge create well being not only for you, but also for others…"

Thank you to Lulu Publishing Services for excellent job in helping to edit and publish this book.

Thanks everyone for joining me on this journey. May light shine brightly in the world around you. God, Bless you!

Non-violence, truth, freedom from anger, renunciation, serenity, aversion to fault-finding, sympathy for all beings, peace from greedy cravings, gentleness, modesty, steadiness, energy, forgiveness, fortitude, purity, a good will, freedom from pride – these are the treasurers of the man who is born for heaven.
The Bhagavad-Gita

Remember that you have only one soul; that you have only one death to die; that you have only one life, which is short and has to be lived by you alone; and that there is only one glory, which is eternal. If you do this, there will be many things about which you care nothing.
—Teresa of Avila

A Far Different Reality

Slava said good-bye to her relatives at the airport in Boryspil. It was especially hard to separate from her only daughter, whom she was leaving with her parents. It was a gloomy autumn day. The sun occasionally peeked through the heavy clouds. It seemed that everything around them was sad, and the sorrowful mood was spreading to the people at the airport.

When the boarding announcement was made, her daughter rushed into Slava's arms and tearfully whispered, "Mum, take me with you."

Some unknown burning pain seized Slava's soul; it was difficult to even utter a word. She hugged her daughter. It seemed that the whole world was begging her not to leave her daughter. But an inner voice strongly ordered, *Go. There is no way back. Your daughter will be with you later; she will be with you again.*

Two conflicting wishes fought within her: the first to remain forever with her daughter in a postcolonial country of the former USSR, and the second to go far away to the New World in search of a better life. The intense desire to live in a free society, where the right to live as she wanted would not be open to persecution, where there would be no fear for the future, no bribery or corruption, where people lived a full life rather than merely survived, was emerging as the preferred choice. It was her dream. She was suffocating in the society where she had been born and raised. Her fragile soul needed to escape; it yearned to be free.

Then came the most painful moment… She tearfully kissed her daughter. Releasing herself from her embrace, Slava approached the airline's registration desk for her flight to New York. While climbing the stairs to board the plane, she turned and saw her dearest relatives, who stood back silently and watched. Her daughter stuck tightly to her grandmother, as if seeking salvation and protection. Slava's father nodded up at her, as if to reassure her that he agreed it was the right thing to do.

Slava advanced another step. Before her, there appeared a wide space, an airfield with several huge white aircraft of different international airlines. It was a remarkable picture that simply amazed her. In her bright soul was born a sense of confidence in the future as well as a majestic pride that she was starting a new life in the free world.

The plane rapidly gained a furious speed and somehow easily winged up into the sky. Below her, the scenes and people retreated; painfully familiar places—the outskirts of Kiev, forests, fields, the huge Dnieper River—dissolved in space and merged together. Slava felt that there was some mysterious connection between it and the land of her ancestors. She considered herself a true Ukrainian, with new views on the modern world that would not have been understood in the post-Communist society. She was interested in the ancient history of Ukraine, the original customs and traditions, the beliefs of old Ukrainians, those who for many centuries and even millennia had resisted foreign invaders and their efforts to erase Ukrainian culture—to erase an ethnic group that inhabits one of the largest areas of Europe, the second largest after France. Somewhere in the depths of her soul, she felt the great injustice and the lie told to ethnic Ukrainians in their native land. But what, in fact, are the roots of the Ukrainian people and the origins of Ukraine? Who are the Ukrainians?

The modern Ukrainians are a Slavic nation in language, and culture. The Ethnic Ukrainians are known for their strong ties to their families and national traditions. It is common for parents, or grandparents to live together with their children and help them to raise their kids. This tradition was a necessity just a couple generations ago when the majority of Ukrainians lived in the villages. Peasant Trypilian costumes still are worn on holidays feature white blouses or shirts, decorated with colorful embroidery. Because of the tradition with the living situations, it is also a Ukrainian custom that grandparents play a great role in raising children. They have a popular saying for this, "Children - our future". Ukrainian people have been known as kind-hearted, friendly, hospitable and well-wishing hard-workers. They are emotional and tend to be open to anything that claims to bring balance and stability in their life. The Encyclopedia Americana stated that Ukrainians are among the handsomest of the many races in Europe and Asia: they are tall, broad shouldered, strongly built; Ukrainian women are noted for their beauty. Ukrainians have rich folk culture, they enjoy music, and many of them perform in choruses and dance groups.

There are many famous Ukrainians who have brought significant contribution to the world. Ukraine has been rich in human talents. The genius who conquered space in 1957 was the Ukrainian Sergey Korolev, spacecraft and rocket designer. The father of rocketry and astronautics, Konstantin Tsiolkovsky, was of Ukrainian ancestry; his ancestor was the prominent Ukrainian Hetman and Cossack leader Severyn Nalyvaiko. Yuri Kondratyuk, a pioneer of spaceflight, was a theoretician and a visionary who, in the early twentieth century, foresaw of reaching the Moon. Ukrainian Valentyn Glushko was the leading Soviet spacecraft and rocket engineer. Igor Sikorsky was an inventor of helicopter and aircraft pioneer in the United States. Microbiologist Ilya Mechnikov was a Nobel Prize winner in Medicine. Mikhail Gorbachev, a Nobel Peace Prize winner, was the last leader of former Soviet Union (his grandparents came to Russia from Ukraine). Oleg Antonov was an aircraft designer and founder of the Antonov, a world-famous aircraft company in Ukraine. Ivan Pulyui was a discoverer of X-rays. Mykola Kybalchich was a rocket science pioneer. Steve Wozniak is an American inventor of Apple Computer and co-founder Apple Inc. (he is of Ukrainian ancestry on his father's side). Martha Stefanyshyn-Piper is an American NASA astronaut. Roberta Bondar is Canada's first female astronaut. Jack Palance (Ukrainian: Volodymyr Palahniuk), an American film actor, was nominated for three Academy Awards. Ukrainian composer Mykola Leontovych is recognized for composing "Carol of the Bells" (Ukrainian: Shchedryk). Milla Jovovich is a Ukrainian-born, one of the best and most successful American actress. Steven Spielberg is a worldwide famous film director and producer, his grandparents came from Ukraine. David Copperfield, an American illusionist, has been described by Forbes as the most successful magician in history; his grandparents were immigrants from Ukraine. Singer Ruslana is the winner of the Eurovision Song Contest 2004. Klitschko brothers are the most famous Ukrainians in the world. Vitali Klitschko, older brother, is the WBC world heavyweight champion. His younger brother, Vladimir Klitschko, is the best Ukrainian boxer. It would require a book to describe all famous Ukrainian people.

Ukraine is one of the new post-Soviet countries on the World map, the exact geographical center of Europe. (Austrian scientists carefully calculated that the precise geographical center of Europe is in the town of Dilove; the obelisk marking the center of Europe is still there today.) Because of centuries of foreign rule, Ukraine is a European nation which is still developing, since independence in 1991. However, the language, culture and history of the Ukrainian people can be traced back at least as far as the 9th century, when Kiev (Ukrainian: "Київ", literally "Kyiv") was already a well-established meeting place of trade routes and nations. Kievan Rus was the largest and most powerful state in Europe. Kiev, the capital of Ukraine, was founded by King Kyi, in the 5th century AD. The Ukrainian legend says that three brothers, Kyi, Shchek and Khoryv, with their beautiful sister Lybid, arrived at the blue Dnieper (Dnipro) River, crossed it and settled on the site of today's Kiev. They named the city in honor of the eldest brother, King Kyi. The Book of Veles (Vles Knyha), written about 875 AD, recounts the history of

Ukraine: this unique book covers more than 20,000 years of ancient history. It records a King Kyi who ruled from 473 to 503 AD which coincides with the founding of the Ukrainian capital city of Kiev in 482 AD. The City of Kiev celebrated the 1500th anniversary of its founding in 1982 although according to archeology, people were living there thousands of years before the traditional date of 482. The Medieval Kingdom of Rus had several famous Kings such as Oleh, Sviatoslav, Volodymyr, Yaroslav Mudryi (Yaroslav the Wise), Volodymyr Monomakh (an ancestor of Queen Elizabeth II) and Danylo Halytsky. Kiev princesses became queens of France, Norway and Hungary.

The available archeological evidence suggests that roots of the Ukrainian people are found in the highly developed Trypillya culture (5,000 - 7,000 BC), the earliest European civilization, which left traces in modern Ukrainian culture. Almost 7,000 years ago wheat was being grown in Ukraine and Ukrainian wheat is the ancestor of most of the finest wheat varieties grown today in the world. Archeologists have found that the earliest horse known to be ridden by man was 6,350 years ago near Dnieper River at Dereivka village, in the heart of Ukraine. The classic Greek Meander design (geometrical ornament) goes back only to 3,000 BC. However, the examples of the Ukrainian Meander from Mizyn (Ukrainian village) on a mammoth tusk bracelet are 20,000 years old. This is the oldest meander design in the whole world. This bracelet is an ancient Atlantis intricate design that has been passed down to modern time, and migrated through many cultures; it is a common pattern used in embroidery, fabrics and traditional egg decorating in Ukraine.

The oldest known map in the world, discovered by archeologists, is from 12,000 B.C. and was found in 1966 in Mezhirich, Cherkasy region, Ukraine. This map is portraying the devastating earthquake that preceded the great flood, which destroyed Atlantis.

The oldest known house in the world is a remarkable dwelling found near Kiev, the capital of Ukraine. It was found in 1965 by a Ukrainian farmer. This house was made of mammoth bones and was built about 15,000 years ago.

The earliest known musical instruments, according to archeologists also were found in Mezhirich, Ukraine. They were made of decorated mammoth bones. The Scythians 2,500 years ago used the bones of eagles and vultures to make excellent flutes.

If accept the theory that any event on the territory of a country is a part of its history, then the roots of Ukraine and its culture go back over 40,000 years according to archeological evidence. The leading scholars in the free world placed the origin of Slavic nations and Indo-Europeans on the territory of Ukraine. (There are eleven Slavic nations: East Slavs – Ukrainians, Belarusians and Russians; West Slavs – Poles, Czechs and Slovaks; and South Slavs – Bulgarians, Serbians, Croatians, Macedonians and Slovenes.) The Encyclopedia Americana located the original Indo-European homeland in Ukraine: "Linguistic and ethnological evidence, tend to indicate that the early home of the Slavs was in the region north and east of the Carpathian Mountains east of the Vistula River and in the upper basins of the Dnieper, Dniester and Bug Rivers." (vol. 23 p. 532). The ethnic Ukrainians are an autochthonous, because there is no evidence that they immigrated to Ukraine from any other lands. The ancient Ukrainians have been described as the first Europeans. American anthropologist, Prof. Richard G. Klein of Stanford University stated that man has lived in Ukraine 100,000 years, and according to the most comprehensive work in English on Ukraine, published by University of Toronto Press - Encyclopedia of Ukraine – 300,000 years.

The former Soviet government was hostile to Ukrainian language, history and culture (the Soviet Union was an empire, but Ukraine and Russia occupied different places in the imperial structure: Ukraine was the object of imperial rule, and Russia was the subject of that empire – the metropole). There was genocide of Ukrainians in the past century. The forceful agricultural collectivization and artificial famines, as a part of the collectivization policies of the Soviet government, killed millions of previously independent peasants and others throughout the country. Even today Russian politicians have claimed that the Ukrainians are not a nation but only a variation of Russians, they forcibly imposed names such as "Little Russians" (Malorussians) or "South Russians" on the Ukrainians. American anthropologist William Z. Ripley in his book "The Races of Europe" stated in comparing the stature of Russians and Ukrainians: "Above Moscow and Kazan, the adult males are two inches shorter than in Ukraine about Kiev" (p. 348). It is ironical that the Russians officially labeled the Ukrainians "Little Russians" although the "Great Russians" as they called themselves, were much shorter in stature.

The origins of Russia are different from Ukraine. Russia, in spite of the similarity of its name in English to the Ukrainian name

Rus, but in Russian it is Rossiia, traces its origins most directly to Suzdal and Moscow (founded in 1147 AD) which were provincial cities under the rule of the Ukrainian capital city of Kiev, and the population of these northern colonies of Rus mainly included Finno-Ugrians, a people who adopted the language and culture of the powerful Kievan Rus in the 11th century, as well as the name of the Kingdom of Rus [Rus is an old native name of Ukraine, the word "Russia" was formed from Rus]. The pressure of Russification (the policy of Russian Empire) over the last 350 years has meant that many Ukrainians have been assimilated into the Russian nation. Many Russians have typical Ukrainian names, which reveal their ancestral origins in Ukraine.

Kievan Rus was a bulwark of European civilization, a sort of its easternmost Ultima Thule, at the edge of the Great Steppe, which was roomed by nomads who kept making incursions into the Ukrainian-Rus lands, some of which were widely disruptive and destructive. Kievan Rus was destroyed in Tatar-Mongol invasion of 1237-1241. After about three quarters of a century of Mongol rule, Ukraine came under Lithuanian rule after 1320, and then under Polish rule in 1569. Polish rule was oppressive and in 1648 Hetman Bohdan Khmelnytsky, prominent Cossack leader of Ukraine, defeated the Polish armies and established an independent Cossack Ukraine. Unfortunately, in January 1654 he agreed to the Pereyaslav Treaty with Moscow which led to the eventual loss of independence, opened the door to Russian domination of Ukraine until 1918. Three years of independence 1918-1921 ended with Soviet Ukraine under Russian rule until August 24, 1991 when Ukraine finally achieved its independence. In spite of a turbulent and dramatic history, Ukraine preserved a cultural constant from the early times of its existence. Book printing began in Ukraine in the 16th century and the first establishment of higher learning – the first not only in Ukraine, but in the whole of the Eastern Europe – Kyiv Mohyla Academy. Notwithstanding its colonial status, Ukraine had wide spectrum of art and literature, mainly – folklore, a vibrant and rich pre-Christian mythology, folk custom, music, songs and dances. Ukrainian history is very unique. The story of Ukraine is intersected by the history of its many neighboring countries, because of this Ukraine has experienced many changes throughout its history, yet it has still maintained a certain national identity that makes it distinctively Ukrainian. The history of Ukraine was written by foreigners. They created their own theory of Ukrainian's origin, which didn't accurately reflect real historical facts. This feature became the source of numerous debates around Ukrainian history. One can discuss, one can argue, but the past cannot be changed…

Because of the challenges Ukrainian people have been historically faced, they are survivors. The total population in Ukraine was last recorded at 44,854,065 in 2013. That means that during the past 20 years, the population of Ukraine actually decreased by more than seven million people. There are many reasons which can be listed as causing the population drop in Ukraine. One fact is that Ukraine is experiencing a new and difficult period of its turbulent history. After the collapse of the Soviet Empire, the rules of life had suddenly and dramatically been changed. Many Ukrainian people have been plunged into poverty; older people have been hit the hardest. According to the University of Michigan's World Values Surveys, Ukraine occupies 78th place for the level of happiness, which means that Ukraine has the lowest index of happiness. The last place 79th goes to Zimbabwe, and Ukraine is next to last. There are no words to express concern and disappointment... People need stability in their lives and everybody tries to look for it in his own way. That's why Ukraine experienced such a large-scale emigration of workers.

There are only 34 million native Ukrainians living in Ukraine today. Another 20 million Ukrainians live in 46 different countries of the world. The largest Ukrainian community outside of Ukraine is in neighboring Russia where about 3 million ethnic Ukrainians live. There are almost 2 million Ukrainians living in North America, with approximately 890,000 in the United States and more than one million in Canada. Many people in Ukraine have hope that tomorrow will be better than today... While Ukrainians look to the future, they are still prepared for tough and uncertain times...

Slava had a dream during her flight; the dream was like a tape of a familiar film from her happy childhood. She was residing in a quiet town in the western part of Ukraine, where ancient customs and traditions of the Ukrainian people were kept. She saw a clear image of her mother, who was a genuine *Berehynia (hearth-mother, protectoress of the clan in Slavic mythology; 'medicine woman' is used in North America among Native Americans).*

In Slava's dream, her mother was like the ancient goddess Tapita, keeping her family in warmth and comfort, or an ancestor of the ancient Ukrainian mother Lel', who was given the Holy Mother's love and could create a healthy atmosphere in the family, teaching her children to love justice, kindness, family customs, and traditions, to honor her relatives. In the dream her mother also sang Ukrainian folk songs. It seemed that it was not she who was singing, but her beautiful soul. It was as if there was no song her mother did not know. Slava picked out melodies on the piano, and her mother sang. She taught Slava to sing duets with her. Her mother told her that during difficult and lonely times when living away from home, the best remedy for the soul is a Ukrainian song.

Before she left, Slava had carefully put a homemade *rushnyk*, traditional wedding decorative towel, embroidered by her mother and an embroidered shirt in her suitcase as charms to take with her so that she would not forget her native roots. According to old Ukrainian customs, a mother protects her children in this world—there is always an invisible connection between a mother and her children.

Her father had taught her to love world literature. Slava was allowed to read all of the books in her home library. She especially loved to listen to her father's lectures on literature. He often organized literary evenings in the school where he taught for many years. Slava often recited the poems of Lesya Ukrainka (the foremost woman writer in Ukrainian literature), Taras Shevchenko (the most revered cultural figure of Ukraine, poet and artist), Ivan Franko (the best known Ukrainian poet and writer), and other authors for him. She was a capable and talented girl.

Slava graduated from secondary school with the highest honors: she received a gold medal (awarded for exceptional scholastic achievement). This award entitled her to enter any higher educational institution in Ukraine without entrance examination. Her parents wanted their daughter to become a doctor because Slava's mother was a pediatrician, but she entered the Taras Shevchenko Kiev State University Journalism Department, from which she graduated with honors. She combined her journalistic work with teaching at her alma mater. She was the youngest teacher there. At twenty-four, she taught the Ukrainian language to first-year students. It seemed she had everything an ordinary person needed for a happy life. She had a good family and a good job…

Then the events came that altered the history of her country. Ukraine, as a result of the referendum in 1991, became independent. It was a great shock to the Ukrainian people. There was a renewed sense of national pride, and an awakening curiosity, as people started to access the truth about Ukraine's history that had been kept in the dark for centuries. Information was finally becoming available. Ukraine had been enslaved for more than 300 years by the Russian Empire and the Soviet regime. The history of Ukraine was muddled up intentionally so Ukrainians would not have a historical memory of their state. The colonizing powers had wanted to make all Ukrainians into a single Soviet nation that stretched across the empire. There was such a state. US President Ronald Reagan had called it "the evil empire"—the USSR. All of that disappeared in an instant. Indeed, it was a great miracle. From one day to the next, Ukrainians woke up in another state.

The national patriotic movement came to Ukraine. Organizations were formed to protect the rights and freedoms of Ukrainians. For the first time, criticism of the Soviet occupation of Ukraine was openly covered by all media. In addition, reports were made that exposed Stalin's repressive policies and the *Holodomor* (Great Famine). The reliable academics estimated place the number of Ukrainian victims of starvation at 7 million to 8 million. That starvation was artificially induced is beyond dispute. The famine was a clear result of the fact that between 1931 and 1933, while harvests were precipitously declining, Stalin's commissars continued to requisition and confiscate ever-increasing quantities of grain, much of it exported to Western Europe. Ukrainian peasants were shot and deported as rich, landowning "kulaks". This dark event, which rivals in its magnitude the Jewish Holocaust, is still largely unknown… The World Encyclopedia stated, "In Ukraine, as in other parts of the former Soviet Union, the Communist government severely limited cultural and political activity… Hundreds of thousands of Ukrainian were sent to Siberia and Central Asia for resisting the government take-overs. During the 1930's, crop failures and government seizures of grain resulted in millions of deaths from starvation…" (1979, vol. 20 p. 6). The systematically organized famine had as its objective the destruction of a nation, whose only crime was that it was striving for freedom… Ukraine had come under the impervious rule of Moscow and the communist regime against her will. Disclosure of the crimes of Stalinism and the Soviet regime in Ukraine became the focal points of progressive politicians, writers, and researchers.

Slava researched the stories of Ukrainian writers who were killed for their beliefs during Stalin's regime between 1920 and 1930. She traveled to Moscow to study the archival information not available in Ukraine. The books of all repressed Ukrainian writers were in a special department of the Lenin Library. It was the largest library of the former USSR. In Moscow, she stayed with the Russian writer Nina Danhulov, whose husband was also a famous author and the editor of *Vsemirnaya Literatura*. This intelligent Russian woman was born in Stavropol, in southern Russia, where an entire village of immigrants from Ukraine – Cuban' Cossacks - still lived peacefully. She knew the Ukrainian language very well, had a sympathetic attitude toward Ukrainian writers, and had often translated their works into Russian.

Slava had spent evenings listening to interesting stories that Nina shared with her. Nina was 64 years old but she looked still as a real beautiful Ukrainian woman - cossachka. She liked to cook traditional Ukrainian dishes. In her cozy apartment in the heart of Moscow, near Red Square, Slava felt Ukrainian hospitality.

Once Nina baked piroshki (stuffed buns) and prepared Ivan-tea in samovar (teapot) especially for Slava. (This is traditional Ukrainian custom: to put the best food on the table and to feed the guests once they have entered home.)

After dinner Nina told Slava about her life, "Do you know, Slava, I was a good friend of Mikhail Gorbachev. My grandparents and Gorbachev's grandparents came to Stavropol from Ukrainian village, Chernigov region…"

Mikhail Gorbachev was the last leader of the Soviet Union who initiated changes known as 'perestroika' and 'glasnost' which melted the rigid Soviet system and liberated 15 republics of the Soviet Union to become independent states, thus ending the existence of the USSR in December 1991. He was awarded the Nobel Peace Prize in 1990.

Nina recalled: "When I was a child, I experienced the Soviet famine of 1931-1933, in that terrible year (in 1933) nearly half the population of my native village starved to death, including my relatives…"

Nina told: "Gorbachev's grandfather, Ukrainian peasant Pantelei Gopkalo was deported and sentenced under the dictatorship of Joseph Stalin in the 1930s on false charges, for being wealthy farmer known as kulak; after enduring nearly two years of torture and imprisonment, he was released; and Gorbachev's paternal grandfather Andrey, Cuban' Cossack, was sent to exile in Siberia for nine years…"

Nina showed Slava photo albums and her books which she translated from Ukrainian into Russian.

Nina said, "I gave Mikhail Gorbachev all books of Ukrainian authors that I translated from Ukrainian into Russian."

Nina found in photo album the picture of her and Raisa Gorbachev. Nina said: "I knew Gorbachev's wife, Raisa Titarenko, as a very intelligent woman. Raisa's father, Maxim Titarenko, a native of the Chernigov oblast in Ukraine, moved to the Altai Krai (Russia) to build railways. Raisa also faced a tough childhood under the totalitarian leadership of Stalin; her grandparents were disposed of their property as kulaks (wealthy peasants), her grandfather was charged and executed; Raisa's grandmother died of sorrow and hunger, her four children were left to the mercy of fate..."

Nina told, "I witnessed the destruction of traditional farming and degradation of villages that caused massive exodus of people from their land and to gloomy industrial Soviet cities, where they were doomed to become brainwashed by communist propaganda and live in small flats under restricting political and economic conditions for the rest of their lives..." Nina said, "You know, Slava, I had everything in my life – joy and sorrow, hard work and nervous strain, successes and failures, poverty, hunger and material well-being..., but, you know, we were happy. Happy with our youth and with our hopes for the future, even just with being alive..."

Slava remembered. Her father told about her family, that during Stalin's collectivization her family like millions of Ukrainians was persecuted because Slava's great-grandmother and great-grandfather were wealthy farmers on their own land. Slava's father told her that Lysenko family was a prominent, influential Cossack family in the history of Ukraine; it dates back to the XVII century. Her ancestor polkovnyk (colonel) Lysenko became the Koshovyi Otaman (Cossack leader, nobleman); he took action in the Ukrainian independence war of 1648 -1654 under the command of Hetman Bohdan Khmelnytsky.

Slava gathered at Lenin Library in Moscow all the information she needed, and wrote her thesis, which she then successfully defended at the Institute of Literature of the Academy of Sciences of Ukraine;

the scientists at this institute have done much to disseminate the truth about the terrible days of Stalinism in Ukraine. They have written volumes that have shed light on previously unknown events during the Stalinist occupation and the suppression of the Ukrainian elites—writers, journalists, academics, and politicians.

Slava witnessed a split in society after independence was announced. She saw that the older generation, mostly Communists, did not perceive Ukraine as a separate entity from Russia. By contrast, the younger generation perceived the change positively. Slava taught the Ukrainian language and literature at Kiev University at the time of Gorbachev's perestroika and saw how the young people were captivated by it. For a while, anti-Soviet and anti-Communist propaganda distracted people from the economic problems, which spread across Ukraine and led to a deeper crisis. People were not paid their wages, pensions, and scholarships for several months. Old economic connections with the former Soviet Union had been destroyed, and it was important to quickly establish a new economic structure to replace the economic dependency on Russia. But instead of restructuring to save the country's economy, the privatization of state-owned property took place with incredible speed. Members of the former local party elite acquired privatized lands, plants, and factories at cheap prices. The state treasury was empty, and there was no money to pay people their salaries. Meanwhile, politicians such as former prime-minister Pavel Luzarenko looted the country (as proved by the American justice system). Billions of dollars were taken out of Ukraine. Corruption and bribery reached its peak during the reign of Ukraine's second president. Like mushrooms after rain, a new group of people united into family clans and formed a still unknown political elite; thus homegrown millionaires, billionaires—the so-called oligarchs—appeared in Ukraine. These thieves still rule the country and today make laws that benefit themselves. They promote themselves to high state positions and bribe the voters... Worst of all, the law of distribution in society was broken. A small group of people robbed a country with a population of 48 million, unlawfully stealing billions while the working population received the minimum wage, fifty dollars per month. In Ukraine a transparent economy didn't exist, there was no open civil society, and corruption was blooming as well as illicit enrichment and criminal behavior. The citizens of the state were deprived of elementary human rights and had become slaves of the criminal system.

Slava was reminded of this sad history affecting her own personal life when she could not even buy milk for her little daughter. She didn't have enough money for cooked semolina with water. She had to feed the child while she was standing in a queue for bread at 7:00 a.m. Her mother had helped. She would bring homegrown fruits and vegetables—mainly potatoes, carrots, apples, and strawberries—and feed the whole family with them. Slava's mother and father also hadn't received their salaries.

But a lucky chance changed Slava's life. When Ukraine became independent in 1991, the borders were open, and foreigners, mainly Ukrainian immigrants from the United States and Canada, started to visit Ukraine. They were thrilled that Ukraine was finally independent. These people saw Ukraine different from its reality; everything that was happening in reality they perceived idealistically. Slava was invited to teach the Ukrainian language at the First International Summer School of the Ukrainian Academy of Sciences of Ukraine. Students of this school were foreigners of Ukrainian origin from England, Canada, America, Italy, and Brazil. For the first time in her life she met people of the free world—free people, who didn't have inferiority complexes and were open in communication. They were Ukrainians, but they were not the same Ukrainians who survived the totalitarian regime of the USSR. They genuinely cared about the problems of Ukraine and would help Ukraine enter into a civilized new world. They were simply well-educated people, and you could see that they were from a better world. It was interesting to talk to them and just to be in their company.

Slava was a beautiful Ukrainian woman with luxurious braids and big brown eyes. She was one of the best students at the university. Oleh Babyshkin, the oldest university professor, called her Lesya Ukrainka (the best known woman writer in Ukraine) during a lecture on Ukrainian literature; he said that her personality embodied the best qualities of a Ukrainian girl. After graduation from the university she was offered work as a teacher of the Ukrainian language by a professor, Alla Koval, head of the Journalism Department. Dr. Koval said she had ability and a talent for teaching, which she had inherited from her father. Students simply fell in love with her, but she was always reserved and treated others with understanding. It was the ideal Ukrainian woman who fascinates others with her extraordinary beauty, her manner of behavior, gentle nature, and ability to see and feel the world as it is, in all its grandeur and beauty.

When she started working at the university, a first-year student fell in love with her. She taught the Ukrainian language in the evening school and returned home at ten o'clock in the evening. The student accompanied her home almost every night and read her his poems, which he dedicated to her. Slava noticed the outstanding abilities of this student of literature and encouraged him to write poetry. Later on he published a collection of poems and became a talented journalist.

Among the foreign students in the First International Summer School was Ray Lapika, an American writer and lawyer. He liked the young teacher's style of teaching. He did not speak Ukrainian because he was born in America, in the state of California, to a family of Ukrainian immigrants. He had studied at Columbia University, worked as a lawyer for many years in New York, and owned his own radio station in California. He was seventy two years old when Ukraine became independent, and he decided to visit his parents' homeland, to get to know the still unknown home of his heritage, to learn its language, culture, and history. His idea was that he would go for a short period of time—just two months—to learn to speak the language of his ancestors. Then a miracle happened: he started speaking Ukrainian. He could not believe his success. He was grateful to his "professor," as he called Slava. He had recorded every lecture on his tape player and carefully done his homework.

And then the long-awaited day had come—the day of the party celebrating the end of the session for students of the International Summer School. The president of Ukraine greeted the graduates of this school; the party took place at the Mariinsky Palace. On that day Slava was dressed in traditional clothes: a snow-white shirt embroidered in red-and-black and a skirt of homemade canvas. She surprised the audience with her charm and Ukrainian beauty; everybody wanted to take a photo with her. Ray Lapika came up to Slava and quietly said, "You are the most beautiful woman—a real Ukrainian. Such people as you can be proud of Ukraine." Slava modestly thanked him for his compliment and approached the group, where her former students were joyfully talking in different languages. Most of all you could hear the Ukrainian language, even with an accent, but they spoke a language that had become native to them. They asked Slava to sing, like she had during the Ukrainian language classes, where Slava taught them to sing "*Oh u luzi chervona kalyna*" ("Oh, in a meadow red viburnum"). And she sang. Everyone suddenly joined in and the whole room filled with the lovely singing of the Ukrainian songs.

Then all were invited to the banquet hall, where they were treated to delicious Ukrainian food—dumplings with cherries, pancakes with cheese, and various sandwiches. After dinner Slava said goodbye to her students, and she was going to leave when suddenly she saw Ray near the door. He was carefully looking at Slava. She approached him and said, "You were a true student… I advise you to continue to learn Ukrainian in America."

"I want to tell you that you are the best professor I have met in my life, and there is no substitute for you… My wife, Halia, sang as well as you do. She left us, went into eternity two years ago. She came from a Ukrainian family named Shcherban who settled in

Canada. I want to establish a scholarship fund in honor of my wife for talented students in Ukraine."

"I like your idea. I see you are not only an exemplary student, but a real Ukrainian."

"Thank you for your kind words, but I am a real American. We lived our lives there, in America. Like many other children of Ukrainian immigrants, we learned, studied, earned money by working hard—we had our own way of life. We understood that Ukraine is somewhere very far from us, under Soviet occupation, and that such a Ukraine that our fathers dreamed of did not exist."

"But now things have changed in Ukraine. Why not help to realize the dream of your parents and move to Ukraine?" asked Slava

"I understand your question… I am a person from another world. For me here, there is much I do not understand. I have questions about why people adapt so easily to any circumstances. Why they think that freedom will fall from the sky. You must fight for it, to defend your rights. I noticed that many Ukrainians are influenced by Communist propaganda. A couple of generations must pass before they are free people. I will try to help young Ukrainians; they will determine the future of Ukraine. Once I am back in America, I'll organize the Fund to Support the Youth. This fund will facilitate the release of the Ukrainians from the Soviet regime. Do you know, it would be nice if Americans of Ukrainian descent—lawyers, businessmen, economists, doctors, bankers, and teachers—came to Ukraine and helped to build the Ukrainian state, and to send young Ukrainian people to America to study. When they return, they can become presidents and ministers. Do you know, Ukraine has to be built by free people..." Ray nodded, studying Slava's face.

Slava's eyes widened. "I see you are an idealist... But your dreams are beautiful. I hope they come true."

"I would like you to support this project and help me realize my dream. For me your support means a lot," said Ray

"Well, I will be pleased to assist you in this project to be realized. I agree with your statements that only free people can build a free and independent Ukraine," Slava said.

"Thank you. Sorry, but I want to tell you that such a woman as you are, I have not seen in my life. I propose you to be my wife and go with me to America."

Slava was stunned by this unexpected proposal. She could only look respectfully into the eyes of this older man as he gazed at her with great trust, like a child looks at his mother when he has done wrong and pleadingly asks her not to punish him. She didn't have the courage to say no, and silently dropped her eyes and headed for the exit.

Slava went home, thinking about how to behave in such a difficult situation when she knew what to say in response. She did not want to offend this elderly man. She didn't have a thought to marry him. She had her own family, and her family life was not going well. She was waiting for a divorce from her husband, raising her daughter on her own. Her parents helped, because Lelya was only five years old.

At home her mother and daughter were waiting for her. Her mum baked delicious pies with apples. Lelya surrounded herself with books and carefully read some stories. She already knew how to read, and loved it when Slava told her something interesting before bedtime. Having breathed in the smell of her mother's pies, she felt the bliss of home comfort. She did not want to think about something that worried her. That what she experienced today had disappeared and that the next day would bring new challenges, joys, and disappointments in this life. But it was more disappointments…

For teaching the foreign Ukrainians, she had been promised 250 rubles. This was a great help, because for six months she had been working without receiving her wages. At the same time she was frustrated, because while talking to foreigners, she realized that her work paid peanuts. Obviously, before teaching the foreigners, she, like other teachers, was given instructions: the teacher must give only positive information about Ukraine, and after the lessons she was to avoid any contact with foreigners.

One day a professor from the University of Manitoba in Canada, who attended Slava's lectures, asked her during a break how much she got for her work at the university. Slava said that for several months, just as other teachers, she had not received anything. Surprised, he asked, "And what do you live on?"

"My parents assist me, my mother brings food from the cottage… and we live somehow…" Slava herself was embarrassed, really, by how she and many like her in this country survived somehow. She had not thought about it previously. It had become a common phenomenon.

"But it's wrong. Why should you and the Ukrainians like you not strike? Why do you not fight for your human rights?" asked the professor.

"Ukrainians are patient people. They survived a lot and they think that everything is temporary and will change for the better. Most important, we live in an independent Ukraine."

"Maybe you're right, but to me it is hard to understand… I live in Canada. In our country the government would not let anything similar happen—for their people not to get paid for months. And yet, what is your wage as a university teacher?"

"I get a hundred and twenty-five rubles," Slava replied.

"An hour or per day?" asked the professor.

"Monthly."

"It is in terms of dollars—you get about twenty dollars?"

"Yes."

"A professor in America or Canada receives two to three thousand dollars per month, and per hour he makes from twenty to thirty dollars."

"I find it hard to believe that I make as much in a month as you make in an hour," Slava said.

"You know, Professor, I listened to your lecture. You have good knowledge of the Ukrainian language, and you use excellent methods of teaching. You could teach in any university in the world. I could help you."

Slava for the first time heard that in the free world she could earn a decent salary and that her work was highly appreciated by the professor from Canada. She could teach the Ukrainian language in any public university in the world. She thought the perfect world actually existed—someplace she could only dream of… She was lucky to get to know the people who thought the other way, who were of Ukrainian origin and, above all, were successful people for whom the norm of life was high humanism, honesty, fairness, and openness.

And now, high in the sky over the waters of the Atlantic, Slava recalled with appreciation these remarkable people whom she had met and who had changed her destiny. She promised to forget the people who tried to prevent her from leaving Ukraine. She wanted to leave it behind, and still she was oppressed by the thought that people in Ukraine were not free yet. There were unpleasant memories of how she had been watched as she worked with foreigners in the International Summer School. She recalled Ray Lapika, who said you needed to change a generation before fear disappeared in the minds of people and revived the instincts of free people… Oh, it could be great if there were more noble men such as Lapika, then the idea of educating Ukrainian youth in the best universities of America would have worked… You know, good stuff would have come as a result of young people studying in the West, free from stereotypes of Soviet thinking.

Ray didn't call Slava in the days after their conversation at the ceremony. Then suddenly, a week later, he called and told her he wanted to visit her with his niece, with whom he had come from Ternopil. He would be leaving for America the next morning, so it was important to meet with Slava that day.

Slava dictated her address over the phone, and an hour later they were at her home. Slava quickly cooked pancakes for tea and treated the guests to homemade sweets. They were hungry and ate all the delicious food that Slava put on the table. Ray explained that they had spent all day in the US Embassy in Kiev, where they met with the ambassador and received a visa for his niece so she could visit America. They did everything successfully in one day, including booking a plane ticket to New York. Their tired faces radiated joy. Slava was pleased to meet these happy people in her home. They stayed overnight in Slava's flat, (rooms were open because her daughter and parents were away in the suburbs). Summer vacations were coming to an end, and it was time to harvest. Slava also was going to go to the village to help her mother collect potatoes. But she stayed in Kiev just to collect her salary at the Academy of Sciences of Ukrainian for her teaching in the International Summer School.

After dinner, Ray said that Zoryana, his niece, was going to America to study. For Slava, it was a pleasant surprise, and she expressed her support for his good intentions:

"This is the first time in your life you visited Ukraine, and you had so much to do: you learned the Ukrainian language, visited your family, made it possible to send your niece to study, and made plans to create a fund for young Ukrainians, so that Zoryana will be the first who goes to study."

"Yes, we must hurry, because people are not aware that life is so short and we need to do too much… especially when you feel that you can change many lives for a better future. My relatives from Ternopil told me how they live… Do you know, I was impressed. They never asked me for help. I had no idea about this injustice that people are deprived of basic human rights, and they have grown used to this life. Zoryana's father is a surgeon at the hospital in Ternopil, and his salary is so small that our doctors earn as much per day as he earns in a year. He cannot afford to buy a car or live in a nice flat. His wife, Zoryana's mother, died two months ago after a long illness. They had no money to take her for treatment in another country. I decided to help this family. Zoryana has a younger brother who stays with his father."

"Do you know, Ray, almost all Ukrainians live like this, except a handful of people with criminalized minds who hold senior positions in government and acquire their wealth on the poverty of Ukrainians by not paying them wages, by opening their accounts in foreign banks."

Ray spoke. "What I saw in Ukraine, having learned about the lives of my relatives—it is called in one word: slavery. Ukraine needs new people, political leaders who would live by the interests of the people, not their personal interests. Ukrainians should get rid of the stereotypes of Soviet thinking and borrow the best that is in the West—democratic values and high humanism.

"Take, for example, the US Constitution, which was written by John Adams. They say he had Ukrainian roots. This is the best constitution throughout the free world that protects human rights. You know, America has the most perfect system of government, exercised through the legislative, executive, and judicial branches. And to breach the highest law—the Constitution—is the greatest crime, even for the president of the United States... All people in America have equal opportunities, all are equal before the law, and nobody is prosecuted for their views, religion, or nationality. So I would like to see young Ukrainians who go to America and study at the universities return to Ukraine and introduce the values of American democracy back home.

"Ukraine has only begun its journey to independence, and you, Slava, would also begin your journey to a new life. Go to America and write a book for young Ukrainians, because not everyone can go there. I can see now that many Ukrainians are interested in going to America to work and make money just to survive. But there is something above money: human values that cannot be bought for any money... Ukraine needs people with a sense of responsibility for the fate of their country, people who are born with a sense of dignity, a sense of obligation to the future generations... These people have to create the Ukrainian elite, and we have to elect presidents and ministers from these people."

"Do you know, Ray, what you have just said struck me. You have lived all your life in America, but you are still taken over by the fate of Ukraine. If Ukrainians had such beliefs, life would be completely different. There is no elite in Ukraine that is interested in preserving Ukraine that takes care of its people, putting love of nation above individual gain. And young people are more interested in how they can earn more money and looking for any opportunity to go abroad, where they can find a good life. Many people do not believe they can live a good life in Ukraine. People are frustrated... frustrated with an established criminal system that has no analog in the world—a system that wants Ukraine to roll into the abyss. Future models are not created. In one word, our fate is disorder.

"Who can feel happy in such a degraded, immoral society? The authorities are the same ones who were there yesterday. The Soviet leaders were not ready for a new wave of time because of their Soviet mentality. But they have adapted in that way and begun to privatize state properties at the lowest cost—for pennies, using their official position. Even in the press we have developed a popular word: *prykhvatization*. Thus there are homegrown millionaires of former party leaders, who assign factories, plants, and land to themselves. They acted very quickly and were well organized and created family mafias, and even children know that there is a Donetsk mafia... They created a criminal system that allows them to legally enrich themselves, and in which there is simply no place for decent people—they are not protected in this country. Everywhere, you meet bribery, corruption, and a fear that you may lose your life if you are against this corrupt government. So lots of people leave Ukraine—they just can't live and provide basics to their family in this dirty, demoralized society.

"I would say Ukraine is a state of the mafia in which a handful of people subordinate everything in this country for their own interests, especially enrichment... The money they take from the Ukrainian people by not paying monthly wages they transfer abroad to foreign banks and offshores. They are like parasites that bite into the body of the Ukrainian people and drink their blood. And people keep silent, because a fear exists in this country, disbelief that something can be changed."

"Slava, you know, all is temporary on this earth, and with time everything will change. Only young people like you can change life in this country. You are a proud and beautiful Ukrainian girl, and Ukraine belongs to you. I will try to help you. But you have to go to

America to a new world and promise me that you will write a book to help teach the Ukrainian language to the rest of the world in all its grandeur and beauty, and give them confidence in tomorrow. The word of a true writer has great power."

Early the next day, Ray and Zoryana were waiting for a taxi at the entrance to her building. When they departed, Slava entered the room where the guests had slept, and saw an envelope and a folder on the table. At first she thought Mr. Lapika had forgotten them. But she read her name on the envelope. She realized it had been left for her. The envelope was full of money: $2,000. In the folder were poems dedicated to Slava that Ray had written over the last two months, while he studied at school, and a short letter in which he wrote that this was a reward for good Ukrainian language classes. The letter ended with the words "We are waiting for you in America."

Slava was impressed with Mr. Lapika's generosity. She had never in her life had such an amount of money. She could not believe that one man was able to earn the money that now belonged to her. She even thought that Ray had forgotten the money. But on the envelope he had written her name. And in a letter he mentioned leaving the money for her. She was confused… Then she remembered that the new academic year was to start in just one week. She had promised her parents she would come to the country. Yes, she would go today. Then in her mind a thought suddenly appeared: *I should go to America*—a place where an ideal world is existed that she should see for herself. There was something there that was not in Ukraine: freedom, justice, equality of people… She was missing Ray and

Zoryana after they departed, and she fiercely wanted to go after them. She remembered how Ray had asked her to write a book, a special book for the Ukrainians. And she would write it, only later—after seventeen years of her life in America.

Unexpectedly Ray called her a week later. Slava had just returned home with her daughter and parents, their bags full of vegetables and fruits grown in the country. She had not expected Mr. Lapika to call her so quickly. Over time she spoke with Zoryana, who enthusiastically told Slava how she was surprised to see New York and its tall buildings... and then San Francisco, where she was studying. In a few days they would be heading to Los Angeles.

Slava told Ray she had decided to go to America, and when she talked to her parents about it, they agreed. But they said she should go without her daughter first. They would consider her later when Slava was firmly settled there.

Mr. Lapika said Slava could come to America as an accredited journalist from the Ukrainian newspaper where she published her articles, and he promised to provide her a supporting letter as a sponsor. For this she needed to take the editor accreditation letter and go to the American embassy to get a visa and a letter from him, as a sponsor, which he would send to the ambassador.

The next day Slava went to the editor of the Ukrainian newspaper *Youth of Ukraine*. The editor sat in his office and carefully worked on a new layout for the newspaper. He was not like other editors of Ukrainian newspapers; he was a man with a new way of thinking.

In many ways they were associates, and she considered him a friend. Slava was sure he would print some articles about America.

When Slava told him that she wanted to be a newspaper correspondent in America, he carefully looked at her... He asked whether she was serious about it or just joking. Slava said it was a very serious request and that she would send some interesting articles about life in America, about this unknown world that had been banned before —a world about which Ukrainians didn't know the truth, having been taught by way of Soviet propaganda that it represented "decaying capitalism." She also said that a former student of the International Summer School, an American of Ukrainian descent, Mr. Lapika, agreed to sponsor her stay in America, and told him about the letter he had sent by fax to the US ambassador.

The editor silently pondered, and then said he had returned from America only three days earlier. He had gone there on a business trip to see and to interview a very interesting Ukrainian man who wanted to change this brutal world.

"Here in my next issue you can read about him," said the editor.

"I would be interested to meet with this person out there in America," Slava said.

The editor shook his head. "Well, I believe that the matter of accreditation is sorted. I will write you a Letter of accreditation and will give you the phone number and the address of this phenomenal man, a great dreamer of our time, living alone in the Catskill Mountains in New York State... He gave me a book called *Maha Vira (The Great Light of Liberty)*, which he wrote. It can take a few days to read, but I will lend it to you if you promise to return it to me, because it means a lot to me. Come back tomorrow, because today I am very busy. The letter will be ready.

"I will phone the American Embassy and ask how to arrange accreditation for someone to work in another country. Previously, we have reprinted the articles about America from the Russian news agencies that were Soviet when the Soviet Union collapsed; the heir of all information agencies was Russia. You see, they had their correspondents abroad and prohibited us… We had no right to be such people as they are. We actually impose anti-American propaganda… I will collect some copies of our newspaper that you can take with you. Come tomorrow, Slava". She looked at the editor, shaking her head. Slava walked quickly out of the room, down the stairs, and out of the publishers building.

Slava went home and immediately began to read the book by the mysterious writer. She could not take a break from this very interesting book; there was so much wisdom… There was so much that Ukraine and Ukrainians could learn from this unique book. She read until the morning, and as she read, her eyes opened as though she were in a new world—the unknown world of truth, which had been hidden from the Ukrainians for centuries… She decided to meet with the author of this great book in America, the man who had ancient knowledge about Ukraine, had supernatural powers, and was a spiritual teacher of the Ukrainian Native Faith.

It took her just three days to settle the case of accreditation. A week later, she booked a ticket to New York. Before she left, Mr. Lapika called. He was very glad to hear that the matter of accreditation had been sorted out successfully. He gave her the contact numbers of his friends, as well as the one for his office, Lapika Law Firm, in New York.

The flight across the Atlantic lasted ten hours. But for Slava the flight felt very short, like one hour, for she plunged herself into memories of the past and did not notice when they announced the landing at Kennedy Airport in New York.

It was a mild, sunny September day, a day she remembered forever. It was a strange feeling when she left the plane and set foot on American soil. It felt like she had been there before, like it was a familiar place for her… She felt some light, bright aura around her. The people around her were hospitable—they smiled, greeting her with a welcoming "Hi."

Slava was watching with interest: it seemed to her that she had landed in an environment close to her people. Everywhere there was affection, kindness. At every step she could hear, "How can I help you?" No one here would bully her or use foul language; everywhere it was very simple and comfortable, as if it were another civilization and an entirely different culture. Even the way of communication and human behavior was different. There was an atmosphere of perfect human society, where human dignity was number one…

Slava involuntarily recalled the words of Mr. Lapika, who had told her that he wanted to help many Ukrainians come here to study—give them a chance to see and know the world, which was considered the most attractive and perfect, an example of the highest development of modern civilization… It was very sad that Ukrainians did not understand where they lived. They didn't understand the distorted relationship between people, how demoralized a society could become in a country where bribery, corruption, blackmail, intimidation, persecution for the truth—the norm of life of millions of Ukrainian people—were widespread... She could not believe such different worlds could exist on one planet. She wanted to know the answer... Why and again why?

Suddenly her thoughts were interrupted by a dark-skinned man in a special uniform, an airport employee:

"Are you okay, pretty girl?" he asked.

Slava smiled to the friendly man and responded with a nod that she was all right. She realized that people here did not show sad moods in public; they were smiling and happy with their lives. The rule: think positively, even if it is difficult.

"And where are you from?" asked the stranger.

"I am from Ukraine," Slava said.

"Oh, my friend is Ukrainian—he works here. Do you want to meet him? He is not far—in another room," and he showed Slava the direction with his hand.

"Thank you, but I am in a hurry."

"Let's go. I see that no one was here to meet you. You may be in need of help..."

He quickly got Slava's suitcase and they went to another room.

"Hi, Michael," her escort greeted a young man who sat in the office of information at the top floor.

"Oh, Jason, what are you doing?"

"Can you see this beautiful girl from Ukraine who got lost..."

"You are from Ukraine? From which city?" Michael said in the Ukrainian language with an accent.

Slava looked at him in surprise and said, "I am from Kiev."

"I was born here. My Ukrainian language is not perfect, but I can understand very well… Is it your first time here? Where are you going now?" said Michael.

"Yes, I am here for the first time in New York, going to Spring Glen…"

"Oh, it is very easy to get there. There is our SUM branch… You should take the express bus to Manhattan and go to the bus terminal at Forty-Second Street, where you change to a second bus, which takes you to Ellenville, but you buy a ticket to Spring Glen, which is very close to Ellenville, and tell the driver to stop in Spring Glen. Here, you go down there and see—there are buses; they depart every thirty minutes to Manhattan"…

"Thank you." Slava took her suitcase and headed for the elevator to go down to the bus stop.

"Good luck," called Michael. "I might see you in Spring Glen…"

Slava waved to him in response.

An hour later she was already in Manhattan. Slava was looking through the bus's window with interest and watching New York. It seemed that the city looked mysterious in the distance—when the bus left the airport, she saw New York in all its grandeur and beauty. She thought that this was the city of the future. She kept it in her memory.

In a large bus station on Forty-Second Street Slava saw a large crowd of people who moved in opposite directions. Everywhere she heard different languages, as in Babylon. She quickly ascended to the fourth floor and bought a ticket to Spring Glen. She had to wait about two hours for the bus. Meanwhile, she went to the Starbucks café. The coffee was good. There was a free newspaper on the table. She took into her hands a copy of the *New York Times.* Thus began her acquaintance with America.

At the bus station she called the teacher from a pay phone. She said she had a letter from the editor and the newspaper *Youth of Ukraine,* which had published an interview with him, and asked if she could come to Spring Glen for a meeting. The teacher replied that he would be very happy to meet with her and added that she would have to ask the driver to stop at a specific address, where he would wait for her.

The journey to Glen Spring lasted almost three hours. When the bus left the big city to get on the highway, Slava looked through the window and viewed New York. She liked the broad, high-speed roads, the buildings grouped around the road (mostly shopping centers), and the small, almost-the-same towns where the bus stopped. Even closer to Spring Glen, Slava saw mountainous terrain covered with forests very similar to the Carpathians. She admired the beautiful landscapes, and of course, thought of meeting with the teacher. The editor had told her he was a person who had knowledge about the world and its origin. He knew about the ancestors of the present and the future of the planet, which in Ukraine was unknown. She wanted to record her very first interview in America with him.

Slava did not notice when the bus drove into a small village in the Catskill Mountains. The bus stopped. Slava saw at the bus stop a man of medium height with gray hair who stood alone near the car. She got off the bus and walked up to him and greeted him. The teacher calmly looked at Slava as if invisible rays of light shone from her. Slava felt warmth and affection toward him straight away. She remembered the light, penetrating glance of his blue eyes.

"Are you Slava?" One could feel a paternal kindness in his voice.

Slava was embarrassed, and calmly replied, "Yes, and my parents called me just Slava."

"It is a very old Ukrainian name that your parents gave you. Do you know where your ancient name comes from?" asked the teacher.

"My name, I think has a common root with the word *Slavs* [in English *Slav, Slavic*], which comes from the words *glorify, nice*."

"Yes, you're on the right road, and all these things come from one word: *word*."

"In the beginning was the word," Slava said.

"That's where the beginning was: the word. It appeared in the first spiritual centers of human civilization... You intuitively feel encoded in the word of information... Now tell me what you intend to do in America, dear Slava."

"I came to discover America, but not as Columbus; I want to learn more about this unknown world and to convey my vision to the Ukrainian people, as they say, from a firsthand point of view. I am an accredited correspondent of the newspaper *Youth of Ukraine*... Oh—most important, I have brought a letter from the editor and the newspaper article of your interview," Slava said excitedly, and pulled the envelope for the teacher from her luggage.

"Thank you very much. You can read this interview for me because my eyes are not so good—the print is very small. I can't see the letters. I understood that you just came from the plane to come to me here."

"Yes, I would like to write about you... I have read your book *Maha Vira*. I'm excited... This is the true book, rich in knowledge unknown to the Ukrainian people. This is the first time in my life I have read such a book."

The teacher said nothing. He took Slava's suitcase and put it in the car. Then he opened the car's door and invited her to sit down.

"First you need to have a rest after your journey. Now we go to the shopping center where you can buy food. There we can have lunch. Then I will drive to the cottage at our church. Nobody occupies it and you can live there. You can live there as long as you want—the owner of the cottage is my assistant, who lives in another state. He comes here only occasionally."

In the giant supermarket Slava saw a huge selection of groceries. She thought that people were buying too much; their carts were full... Slava was confused initially and did not know what she wanted to buy because she was unfamiliar with the groceries. Everything was in bright wrappers, beautifully packaged. There was a great variety of food. In Kiev shops she did not see anything similar to this. She recalled that every morning in Kiev she had to go to the grocery store to buy bread and milk because these products were simply sold out in a few hours. Usually the family breakfast consisted of milk and bread...

The teacher noticed Slava's confusion. She watched as he took a few bagels, a carton of milk, and a package of dried fruit. Slava copied the teacher and also took milk, bagels, and fresh strawberries.

The teacher smiled, and put in a round loaf, a bag of oatmeal cookies, butter, cheese, yogurt, various fresh vegetables, and fruits in the cart. When they approached the cashier, the teacher said, "That's all for you. You do not have to worry; I am paying for it."

Slava did not know what to say. She was still in a state of confusion at what she saw. Its impressive contrast—between what she saw every day in Ukraine and what she saw in this store—did not fit into any frame in her mind.

"Is there something you are worried about, Slava?" the teacher smiled. His voice was very quiet.

A few seconds later, Slava spoke. "Yes. I feel that I am in another world that is so far from where I was before… And this world surprises me with its greatness and simplicity at the same time. There is something incredibly attractive…"

The teacher shook his head. "I understand your feelings. As you can see, America is a country of immigrants from around the world. America has always provided asylum for all those who thirst for freedom; it is a country of human dreams…

"You see, Slava, the life of Americans is established very well; they have everything they need to live a quiet, secure and worthy life. Here, everybody is given equal opportunities. And they are given the equal opportunities by their Constitution, the supreme Law of the land, as they say. There are many contradictions in this country, but ordinary people do not notice them. America is at the top of material civilization. The main factor of it is its material wealth, and the price for living here is simply hard work. In this society a person of labor, the simple worker, is honored.

"The ethnic national groups living in America are strongly supported. There are even entire government educational and cultural programs to promote national communities, involving finances. They call them grants. So take Ukrainians—a large Ukrainian community living in America. They have many different organizations—cultural, religious and business. And they do not have any problems in relation to American society. On the contrary, Ukrainians are respected as a hardworking and good people here. And you'll be able to get to know them. All is yet to come, Slava…"

"I'd love to see how the Ukrainian immigrants live in America," Slava said. "But I am concerned about one question. Why in Ukraine a man is not free, and he lives in constant fear of how to survive? Why am I seeing this amazing contrast—how people should live in the free world and how people should not live in Ukraine?"

"The answer to your question, Slava, is short. The idea is that Ukraine fell under the experiment of building Communism in the former USSR. As you can see, this system has suffered a complete collapse—the Soviet Union collapsed. There was no Communist paradise, and there is not. The utopian materialism there was built from above by violent means; people were pushed by force into collective farms. Those who opposed it were sent to Siberia to live in concentration camps without the right to return home. Many of them were shot. Only after the collapse of the USSR did this information become available to the world.

"And we must remember the Great Famine in Ukraine, organized by the ruling elite of the Soviet Union led by Stalin. These acts are considered in the free world as an act of genocide. We have not forgotten about the political repression of the twenties and thirties of the last century that led to the destruction of the Ukrainian intelligentsia, the intellectual elite, flower of the nation. In the twenty-first century, humanity has learned about the vandalism, the violent extermination of Ukrainians, and the starvation of people by planned hunger. Ukraine experienced the brutal, horrible crimes of Stalinism. This European country became the victim of a criminal Communist regime that was condemned in the world, but not in Ukraine.

"As you know there was a striking inequality in the USSR, with the ruling elite, which had all the privileges and unlimited power. On the other side, you had ordinary people, from whom the elites took everything. You have seen yourself what is happening in Ukraine now. The heritage of the Soviet past has been transmitted to independent Ukraine… It hurts to see this, but Ukraine today is a sick society, imbued with the difficult consequences of the past. You know, if the patient has no faith in recovery, he will never recover. It is the law of Mother Nature.

"Materialism in the West developed spontaneously. It was a free competition, freedom of choice… Today we call it democracy. The advantages that have created this civilization naturally generated a wish to dominate the rest of this world, which in their understanding was considered imperfect.

"As you know, Slava, American society was built by Europeans who fled from their lands in search of freedom, justice, and religious tolerance. However, this land was actually conquered by them. You know from history that America was a British colony and that there lived in the land indigenous tribes of Indians. Now eight hundred thousand of sixty million Indians survived… As a result of the Revolutionary War, America was freed from British oppression and gained independence. This independence was won by the same Europeans who did not want to obey the English monarchy. They have created here a model of a paradise on earth where human community puts economic dependency and spirituality in the context of the framework and conventions of the technocratic world… Soon you will see it yourself. Most important, America has always rejected and condemned Communism as the gravest crime against humanity. Therefore, these are different worlds—America and Ukraine…

"And we have arrived at last," the teacher said, slowly coming through the gate that led to the church. There was a small cottage on their left, very close to the main road. This was the cottage where Slava settled, where she began her journey into a new life on American land.

A Person is Born and Comes Free to this World

"A person is born free into the world. When she was a child, she did not know yet how life will abuse her soul. She did not realize that when she became an adult, she will suffer oppression, abuse or hurt, and the most valuable gift that Mother Nature gave her – freedom - will be taken from her, and she will struggle for the privilege to be free…" These disturbing thoughts appeared in Slava's mind after her night-dream in her first morning in America.

Slava made herself green tea and sandwich but she did not want to eat. She was still thought about the dream that she saw last night… She recalled: in front of her was a river so wide and raging that she dared not step closer or try to cross it. She stood there feeling so helpless and full of despair. She was thinking, "Oh my goodness. What am I supposed to do?" All of a sudden there appeared before her a crystal bridge reaching from one side of the vast river to the other. Then it was as though someone spoke to her, "If you want to be safe you must cross this bridge immediately… The thunderstorm will come soon. It's all going to be destroyed…"

The Price of Freedom

Slava saw on the sky dark clouds and flashes of lightning. She head sounds of thunder. Slava ran over the bridge, and all of a sudden she saw golden wheat sway in the breeze and blue sky above her. The sun shone brightly. She was standing in front of a vast wheat field looking out upon a harvest that was clearly ripe. What seemed like endless acres continued for as far as her eyes could see. The harvest was so plentiful, and she was so excited. Suddenly Slava heard the voice of her daughter, "Mama... mama..." Lelya was running towards her... Slava woke from her dream and realized that this dream was as a prediction of her future.

It was late autumn, but the sun still gave its last warmth before winter. Slava dressed up, put her favorite woolen coat, which was embroidered by her mother, and went to the church. It was not far. She looked at the clear blue sky above her. She saw – wild geese were flying away. Slava walked through the park which was covered with yellow and red autumn leaves. She opened the door to the church and went to the library, which was located right near the entrance to the church. She carefully looked through the books. Slava took one book and read carefully.

Some time later the teacher came into the library. "Good morning, Slava. It's nice to see that you started your day by reading books. What are you so interested in?"

Slava showed the book. It was "Root" by Alex Haley.

The teacher nodded understanding, "You know, Slava, this book changed America... Halley told the story of 39 million Americans of African descent. He has discovered for an entire people a rich cultural heritage of African people that speaks to all races...Haley earned a Pulitzer Prize award for this book He describes the plight of African people who were captured, sent to America in slave ships and sold into slavery... This was despicable. How could human beings do such things to their fellow man?... Give me liberty, or give me death! - is the famous proclamation by the American patriot Patrick Henry. This is the heart's cry of every human being... We ache inside when we hear about the awful suffering of starving people in Ukrainian villages during Holodomor in 1931-1933. It troubles us when we read about Josef Stalin's and Adolf Hitler's concentration camps... Every nation has such tragic pages in their history..."

The teacher spoke deep in thought. "You know, Slava, my life has been one of trials and tribulations. I witnessed the Genocide Famine – Holodomor, and Stalin's mass purges of 1937. My father, Terentiy, was shot by the communists because he was a hard-working farmer on his own land... My family endured brutal persecution by Stalin's regime. I remembered my family was disposed of their property as a 'people enemy', independent farmer known as kulak. During the Nazi occupation I was imprisoned in a German concentration camp, and only the end of the war saved me life. During World War II more than 6 million civilians in Ukraine were tortured to death and 3 million Ukrainians were killed in the war. Throughout the Stalinist era the KGB spent much of its time rounding up supposed 'enemies of the state' to be sentenced for construction work in Siberia... Like many Ukrainians, I emigrated to the West. In 1949 at the Palace of Justice in Paris, France, I gave testimony in the Supreme Court at trial of well known dissident Victor Kravchenko, author of the book "I Chose Freedom". In 1948 all press agencies broke the news about Victor Kravchenko an essential employee of the Soviet embassy in Washington defected. His book in English, French, and Spanish was spreading around the world, telling about Moscow as an empire of evil, terror, violence, concentration camps. In Paris, communist newspapers "L'Humanite" and "Les Lettres Francais" wrote that Kravchenko betrayed the USSR and in his book he maligned the prosperous construction of socialism and the world communist leader Josef Stalin. Victor Kravchenko asserted that he wrote the truth, which could be proved by such witnesses as Ukrainians, Belarusians and Russians, and representatives of other peoples in Eastern Europe. He brought a lawsuit against the said newspapers. Preparation for the Victor Kravchenko court hearing began. Dissenter Kravchenko asked those people who had been to the camps to testify about the NKVD-KGB (Soviet Secret Services) terrors, Holodomor, and concentration camps that were scattered in Siberia, Kolyma, Solovki Isles and throughout the territory of the empire the USSR. Many courageous Ukrainian agreed to testify as witnesses. Apparently, those who feared for their relatives to be persecuted or even killed kept away from the court hearing. Andriy Livytsky, President of the UNR (Ukrainian National Republic) in exile, recommended me to go to Paris to testify in the Kravchenko case that while schoolboy I miraculously survived the famine, that I could testify about eviction of prosperous peasants from their homes, forced deportation of their families… I agreed to testify as a witness. All witnesses were required to speak only about what they saw and felt themselves and answer to the questions posed to them. I was the youngest witness and that brought attention to me at the courthouse. While discussing the Holodomor in Ukraine, an attorney for the French communist party said that Hitlerites (Nazis) wrote a great deal about the famine, and Kravchenko's witnesses read and then had just been retelling what they read. Judge Durkheim asked me how I would respond to that. I said that I saw my mother sick because of hunger, and I saw how those who died of famine were put on a wagon... I said that the lawyer, who claims that there has never been a famine in Ukraine, reminds me a sad story. A father had three sons. When he died, two sons were walking behind the coffin and crying, and the third son was laughing. Everybody knew that the third son was insane... The lawyer's sacrilege over those who died of hunger reminds me of that son who was laughing at his father's funeral... This caused commotion in the courtroom... Newspapers in Paris published my photo and reports about my testimony. Newspaper New York Herald Tribunes, as far as I remember it was No. 20534, wrote article "A Ukrainian left Russia to fight against Soviet Fascism", it was stated that before the war I had been victimized by Russian Communism. Soviet prosecutor Ivan Rudenko was present at the court hearing along with a number of agents who were photographing every witness. One of the agents approached me and asked, "Who is your father? When and where you were born? A Frenchman sitting nearby signaled me not to answer.

"When I was in Paris I had a chance to see the Napoleon's grave and visit museums of French writers Honore de Balzac, Victor Hugo, Guy de Maupassant, Voltaire. I carefully studied their scripts and everything related to the lives of writers, especially I was delighted with writing of Voltaire, he mentioned in his works about Ukraine, and he was a French Enlightenment writer, historian and philosopher famous for his wit, hit attacks on the established Catholic Church, and his advocacy of freedom of religion, freedom of expression, and separation of church and state; Voltaire was a versatile writer, producing works in almost every literary form: plays, poems, novels, essays, and historical and scientific works, he wrote more than 20,000 letters and more than 2,000 books and pamphlets…; as a satirical polemicist, he made use of his works to criticize intolerance, religious dogma…, and we have some of his book in our library."

The teacher spoke again, "I also visited Villiers Abbey where Anna Yaroslavna, Queen of France, was buried. As you know, Queen Anna was the daughter of Kievan Rus King Yaroslav the Wise. Her older sisters became queens – Anastasia in Hungary and Elizabeth in Norway. Anna was a wife of French King Henry the First. She was very educated. The chronicles said, when she came from educated Kiev to Paris, Anna wrote to her father that she lives in a village, where there are no palaces like in Kiev, and it is difficult to find an educated companion… She brought with her to the remotest depth of the provinces, which France was then, a part of the library of her father, some books from which in 19th were found in the library of Mr. Sulakadzaev: it was he who made the first translation of the "Book of Veles", which is a unique original ancient document that covers more than 20,000 years of the history not only Ukrainian but all Slavic people.

"The son of the French Queen Anna, Philip, became the King Philip the First; he was loved by the people and his name was very popular… Frenchmen can honor the makers of French history. I spoke French poorly and therefore tried to speak to Frenchmen in German. I knew that Frenchmen mostly spoke German, but they did not want to speak it in Paris as a matter of principle. The Frenchmen believe that it is not a good morale to speak other's mother tongue in Paris, and especially when the native speakers of that other language used to occupy France… Frenchman is a Frenchman first of all. He is proud of France and its language and history. I liked French people; they enjoy humor and jokes, even though they are neighbors to Germans, very different people. They are more sensitive; they have something characteristic of the Romance peoples. They are Catholic, yet they not emphasize their Catholicism. I recalled I read in Napoleon Museum the following words by the great son of France, Lois XIV: "Neither St. Peter, nor his heirs (i.e. Roman popes) have any authority over the King of France; and the state is completely independent from the church." French people consider freedom and happiness more important to them than money, moral goodness, and even going to Heaven…"

The teacher smiled slightly, shook his head and spoke again, "I remembered, French communist lawyer Jon Vursmer, he was a deputy of Maurice Thorez, the leader of French Communist Party, told me in the courtroom that I was 'a traitor of my Motherland, of the USSR', and that was why I was in Paris as a witness. I responded: 'Great French philosopher Voltaire said that Ukraine had always strove for freedom. I am the son of Ukraine. I am ready to walk up the echaffaut (scaffold) for the freedom of Ukraine.' You know, Slava, these my words were accurately reprinted by all French newspapers. Yet there was newspaper 'Russkaia Mysl' [Russian Thought] published in Paris by Russian monarchists, White Guards who did not recognize such words and concepts as Ukraine, Independent Ukraine, Ukrainian people... So, they printed my photo and wrote what I said as follows, 'I am the son of Russia. I am ready to walk up the echaffaut for the freedom of Russia...'

The teacher smiled and nodded thoughtfully, "I remembered, it was in Bremerhaven, Germany, in 1950. A new immigration law cancelled the visas for hundreds Ukrainian families to immigrate to the United States simply because they were citizens from the Soviet Union. I wrote 'Open Letter to the American people', which was sent to the President of the United States, to Congress, Senate and American newspapers. I declared a seven day hunger-strike, which ended for me in hospital in the city of Augsburg. In a few weeks, after a revision of the controversial immigration law, all Ukrainian families rejected in Bremerhaven received visas, allowing them to immigrate to the USA. You know, Slava, I was so happy that I helped people to be free, to escape them from the horrors of Stalin's reality..."

The teacher took a newspaper from the book shelf and gave it to Slava. The newspaper Svoboda (Liberty, March 9, 1951, Jersey City) featured an article about this event.

Slava read, "Affirmation of Lev Sylenko is the voice of millions. This voice must be remitted to those who establish and effect

American politics today. From this may depend the fortune and even the future of America and of all the Free World…"

The teacher said nothing. He closed his eyes for a long moment. When he opened them, he looked at Slava. Tears streamed down her face…

The teacher was silent for a moment before saying, "My life is not my own. It belongs to my people…"

Slava silently thought, "How great must be a man's love for his motherland if, finding himself separated from it not by choice and having lived through the horrors of Stalin's reality, he forgiven all insults and continues to live and create in its name, in order to cleanse the name of Ukraine from denigration and oblivion, to glorify it in the name of the conscience of historical science, to help it gain its rightful place in the community of nations, to resurrect its values, eternal traditions, culture, morality and ideals… His soul has embraced the pains of Humanity, just as a mother embraces her newborn child. He has appeared at the dawn of a new direction in the history of the world. He bears the sun of the sacred faith, the Great Humanism, which ordains that there be harmony, mutual respect and peace among nations… This Man devoted his entire life to the service of his long-suffering nation, so that it would win freedom and independence and be respected by other nations of the world as an equal among equals…"

The teacher nodded understanding and spoke again, "Look at the French Revolution and how the people got fed up with tyranny. In 1789, they set about to stop it. And the oppression that occurred in Romania is a more recent example of a population that suffered tremendous abuse until they wouldn't stand for it any longer. Romania is a part of Central Europe; it borders the Black Sea and the Danube River, and the history of Romania is intersected by the history of neighboring Ukraine... As generations had done before, they too worked for liberation. This shifts in social order are all proof that no matter how powerful a government or system becomes, people will not put with such ill treatment forever. In each of these cases, there came a time when someone said, 'Enough!' A revolution started, some violent, others more peaceful, and soon had the support of all those with eyes open to see the plight of the suffering masses. Unfortunately, the reality is not so simple... Centuries of oppression are not so easy to overcome. The only weapon that will ever effectively win the war against injustice, slavery, corruption and poverty in Ukraine is the truth. All people need the truth. And when they know the truth, they shall be set free..."

Slava nodded thoughtfully. "Teacher, where is the truth?"

The teacher replied, "In your heart, Slava... Listen to your heart, your intuition, the inner voice of your soul..."

Slava was born in the heart of Ukraine—Kiev, the most beautiful city of Europe. Once upon a time this city had a different name—Sur'yahrad, which means "City of the Sun." Many thousands years ago there lived fair-eyed people of Aryan tribes. They had their own highly developed civilization. But Slava didn't know anything about it, because the true history, original culture, ancient traditions, and native spirituality were hidden from the people. Her soul felt this great injustice, and she had been constantly in search of truth since she could remember. She had been the best student in her school, and learning came easily to her. She was very curious and wanted to know everything that was written in the textbooks and even more. She was different from her peers, asking the teachers questions. They sometimes just did not know the answers. Then Slava would go to the library and looked up the answer in dictionaries and encyclopedias, and books on biology, physics, chemistry, history, and astronomy. She could not find the answer to many questions, but on a subconscious level felt that knowledge of the modern world was less informative than knowledge that encoded the wisdom of our ancestors, with their centuries-old experience—and she sought this knowledge. She asked strange questions: What is life? What is sixth sense? How did man appear on earth? Does Darwin's theory prove the origin of man from apes? Then why are we human beings? Who are our ancestors—"barbarians"? What was our culture like before the adoption of Christianity? Why had people of the white race adopted Christianity more than a thousand years ago? They had had their own vision of the world, which had been formed for millions of years. Where had Aryans, Hyperboreans, Atlantis, Trypilians, and Scythians disappeared to? Why has mankind forgotten the Vedic culture? Why does the history of Ukraine start from the baptism in 988? Does that imply that the Ukrainians did not exist until that time? Why does the science of human history not exist - a science that studies the dead civilizations on our planet? Are people on Earth connected with space? What is an aura, telepathy, clairvoyance? Are there extraterrestrial civilizations? If they exist, why they are not in contact with people of our planet? What is the soul of a man? Does it exist after leaving for higher worlds? Why are people born with supernatural powers? Why can't they accept modern science? Why do people appear in this world free, only to have their minds enslaved by conventions of this imperfect world? Why? Why? Why? And many more of these questions…

Her nature sought higher knowledge than that possessed by modern science. She found that knowledge to be imperishable, the richest treasure on Earth. But she found it not in her native Ukraine, but far across the ocean, by Oriana, the so-called Ukrainian land in New York State where she met a spiritual teacher. There, on Oriana, is the Dazhboh Church (Ukrainian: Sviatynia, literally Holy Place), unique in the modern world, where the teacher lived. This bright man came to this earth to rescue humanity before the threat of its death. By his teachings he warned Ukrainians that if they didn't return to their primary source, to the ancestors' experience, to their native spirituality that had existed in the territory of modern Ukraine (the ancient name: Kievan Rus) more than 1,000 years ago, they faced extinction. He had a few followers who understood him. All of them lived in different states of America and came to the temple several times a year just for special occasions. The teacher lived alone in the church; he called himself *oriyanskyy samitnyk* (Oriana's hermit). Before that, he lived alone in Canada, where he wrote a great book called *Maha Vira* (*The Native Faith*).

In New York State there are many different Ukrainian organizations. Slava met with famous figures, leaders of these organizations, and ordinary people, and wrote articles about them. But few of them knew about the master, and none of her colleagues had such knowledge about a teacher. He said of himself, "I came from the Temple of Ancestors—Trypillya (Tripolye). I wandered fifty centuries…" This man was simple by nature, and perfect. The light radiated from his big, beautiful soul. He was modest and unassuming about material wealth, believing that a man did not need luxury, but only essential stuff to live in harmony with nature, with the universe. When he spoke with the people, he saw every person through as if he had X-ray vision. He could name the person's problem and see the person's past and future, but he did not speak much about it. He had the gift of clairvoyance. His language was simple and concise. It was nice to listen to him. Each word was filled with profound meaning and unsolved wisdom. He was kind and compassionate to people, and he forgave people their imperfections. There was a great spiritual power and nobility in this man of small stature with a correct figure. He was silent and thoughtful. When the teacher told Slava interesting stories about ancient history, she felt like she was in another world—a beautiful and perfect place, where only the highest desires are present. He had a highly developed sense of justice… You could not compare him with someone else. It was as if he had the higher law of being encrypted in him. Perhaps the teachers of mankind—Spitama Zarathustra, Gautama Buddha—were the same.

Slava learned that the teacher restored the Native Faith, which was in ancient Ukraine more than a thousand years ago, before Christianity was introduced by force. He pronounced monotheism in the faith of the ancestors' fathers—the faith in *Dazhboh*, which has no image, no sex, and represents a light, energy of conscious and unconscious being, higher consciousness, love, and harmony of this world. The great book *Maha Vira,* on which he worked as a spiritual teacher for more than twenty years, is about these beliefs. In this book he gathered evidence, proof of his knowledge, in the largest libraries of the world while traveling in different countries in Europe, Asia, and America. And writing this fundamental work was possible only in the West, where an author can be unconventional and have objective approaches to ancient history and religions of the world, such as the traditions and culture of Kievan Rus. The views of most scientists in the West are based on irrefutable scientific evidence and facts, which are impartial and not political. The teacher in his fundamental book referred to that knowledge. This book is the product of heroic research and documentation, containing as it does information about Ukraine, its history and prehistory. It gives a new interpretation of the ancient religion of Rus and of the unknown world of its pre-Christian culture, which had its roots in the Trypilian culture, as described in man's oldest spiritual books, Vedas.

The eminent Ukrainian Humanist, Academician Yevhen Tovstukha wrote: "Maha Vira has as the keystone of its most-humane philosophy the highest virtues of our people and is the majestic heir of the code of wisdom that people created and according to which they have lived throughout the millennia… The Teacher has sacrificed all that he has for Ukraine and Ukrainian people. His thoughts, his inspirations and intuition are synchronized with the cycle of cosmic existence, on which depends the fate of the planet Earth and the vibrations of thought of its restless denizens…"

Slava shared her thoughts with the teacher. She told him that she talked with celebrities both in Ukraine and in the Diaspora (Ukrainian community in the United States) and realized that some of them had read books of the teacher. Strikingly, they agreed that the teacher wrote the truth on the basis of irrefutable evidence and facts, but they lacked the courage to recognize it publicly: it was easier to think as they pleased and to keep it quiet than to try to change the views of the world in this technocratic civilization, even if that meant hiding the truth.

But, in fact, some Ukrainian journalists and scholars openly stated in their publications that the teacher wrote about the causes and consequences of the spiritual slavery of the Ukrainian people for centuries, that the Ukrainian nation has a glorious past, deep historical roots, a unique ancient culture, and one of the most ancient languages on the Earth. Ukrainians have something to be proud of, something to honor—a spiritual holiness of their own. But they had lost these things over the previous millennia. They do not know who they are. Their genetic memory has been taken from them. Until now in Ukraine, the true ancient history of Ukraine, with the Mizyn (Mezine) culture and the Trypillya civilization, has been concealed, and forced baptism was also kept hidden. (Some historical records confirm the facts of forced adoption of Christianity in Kievan Rus.) Still most historians corrupt the historical past of Ukrainians. Slava remembered the favorite phrase of the teacher, "To go forward to the future, we must know our past."

The teacher frequently shared his opinion with Slava about current situation in Ukraine. Once he spoke, "It is a sad. The present Ukrainian generation was brought up on lies in spiritual and political slavery, in the ever destructive energy field. As a result we have our demoralized society in which nothing is sacred, and the ancestors' guidance is lost. People try to adapt, to avoid being slaves to tradition. And such a society is doomed to corruption, extortion, bribery, various kinds of fraud, double standards, harassment and intimidation—in other words, such a society doesn't have a future, but is doomed to extinction. This is the law of the universe. We all live in vibrations with our planet and our galaxy, and if these vibrations do not correspond to the vibrations of the universe, everything that has a negative energy has to die.

Once the teacher said, "You know, Slava, currently in Ukraine there is a fight, only in this country, it is an ongoing fierce fight between good and evil; in the sense of space it means positive and negative energy. Good still lives in the good hearts of ordinary people, and it shows in their best traits—love of their native land and their ancestors, and tolerance toward people of other nationalities and faiths.

"Evil represents the lowest human desire—the insatiable desire for money, fraudulently promoted authority, supremacy up to the devaluation of the lives of others, the parasitic way of life—and that evil became the norm for the ruling elite and today has reached the greatest authority of all time while modern civilization exists. You do not have to calm yourself down by believing that somehow it will exist. It will be like most people wish it. Only people will decide what to think and how to act, and in turn that will determine the direction of civilization on Earth. The people decide the fate of their being, and the fate of future generations is in their hands."

Slava thought for a moment, and then said, "Teacher, now I realized that you came to enlighten people, to awaken them. In your science are encoded healthy grains for survival of the Ukrainian people as descendants of ancient human tribes of the white race."

The teacher smiled a little then said, "But to escape from captivity is very difficult when you do not feel the taste of freedom…"

Slava brightened, "True… I remembered that million of Ukrainian citizens felt it on Independence Square (Maidan Nezalezhnosti) in Kiev during the Orange Revolution of 2004. From many Ukrainians who witnessed these events, I heard that this gift is given only once in lifetime. It was a special feeling, causing you to cry because of the unfathomable joy of realizing that you are a human being, a child of Heaven and Earth – on the planet Earth there is nothing more beautiful than a man; that you have the greatest treasure on the Earth and it cannot be measured by any material values: freedom."

The teacher thought for a while then said, "The Maidan will remain as the square revolution in the history of mankind. But at the center of the square should be not a leader, but a people's council that includes the most respected people from the community (as it was with a council of elders in ancient times). These new people with the new thinking and the will of the ancestors will decide the fate of the nation and its future. Once in ancient times our ancestors called it the Viche, which is the role model for today's Maidan."

The teacher spoke again. "The experience of mankind proves that politics is not a category of good. We must all remember that today it is useless to seek ways to unite the parties in finding a new leader for the so-called "opposition"—the old slave habits and traditions don't end. As always, the first priority will be redistribution of power and competition. And it never stops the chaos and disorder in the country. We must forgive those leaders who did not live up to expectations and in fact betrayed the people in their expressed will. We must recognize that this was an unfortunate period in the history. We must recognize it as a trial, as the experience of this generation that has to become immune to treachery, lies, conformity, and double standards. The second time they have no one to deceive. Most important was the winning of the Orange Revolution. The people at the square for the first time learned that the highest value to humans is their freedom."

Slava agreed. She looked at the teacher for a moment and then said, "It was unforgettable event on the Maidan in 2004, and I did not miss any of the news on American television. They shook the world. No one in the free world in the Diaspora could forget the birth of freedom in independent Ukraine. This day—the birthday of liberty—will remain in the memory of current and future generations."

The teacher frowned thoughtfully, then said, "You know, Slava, there are too many to remember…I hope that the new Ukrainian generations, in whose souls are sown grains of the Maidan, will be proud that they are Ukrainians. When you do not love your native land, you cannot respect other people. This generous feeling brought up from childhood, caught up with mother's milk, and in a society that has such people, the ideal of liberty is created. Everyone is born free, but not everyone has freedom. Mother Nature gives this precious treasure only to those who have an innate instinct for preserving the family, nation, and all humanity."

American Facts, Myths, and Realities

On arrival in the country of your dream after crossing the Atlantic, you begin to realize the vastness and diversity of the American world, the country's endless and the world's best highways, so different and unique with a claim of supremacy, giants cities with shiny, tall buildings up to the sky, a simple and practical underground, giant ports and bridges… At the same time it is a country of small one-story towns with its huge supermarkets and small shops, inexpensive and luxury hotels, excellent restaurants, cheap fast-food cafés. It has countless incredibly attractive national parks, and a variety of entertainment ranging from Las Vegas to Disneyland. There are wonderfully organized recreational beaches in Florida, Virginia, California… What is particularly striking is the contrast between the absolute artificiality of this super-civilization and the incomprehensible eternity of wildlife, which is maintained here in all its beauty and purity. This contrast brings to recollection the high speed of human life—the supremacy of civilization over the natural beauty of this world… When traveling over America on a flight from the West Coast to the East Coast, you see countless lights of small towns and the bright glow of the big cities, like stars and constellations of galaxies forming a mysterious unity of the world.

It seems that everything is created so that a person will have a careless, secure life without any problems. But the most impressive characteristic of this vast country is the organization and unity of all people as one giant organism. All of the above, if contemplated from the outside, will not open you to the real America. This world will soon look strange and cold to you if you do not become a part of it, if you do not know these good, open-minded people who live and work in the developed country. These particular people helped a Ukrainian accredited journalist adapt to the American environment and contributed to her professional work as a journalist of the foreign press. In a short time she felt very comfortable here—not as among strangers, but as among her people. She saw that the life of these people was established and that they had everything, so that they did not need to be angry or envious. In their comfortable life there was almost no place for deception or injustice. And interestingly, their courtesy, friendliness, openness (open minds), and a smile on their lips were seen as daily norms of life. It was something that worked automatically. Without these features, as clearly measured as the mechanism on a clock—living in this country would be simply impossible to imagine. Slava thought that such relationships between people here would be possible in Ukraine only in the future, many, many years later… Obviously, her vision of America was explained by the fact that she looked at this country through the eyes of a

Ukrainian journalist who came here to learn more about this world. Her views may not have coincided with others.

The first city Slava went to was New York. As an accredited journalist who freely obtained the accreditation, she was present at the meeting of the UN General Assembly. Here she saw the leaders of many countries, the president of the United States, and Kofi Annan, the famous fighter for human rights all over the world. She spoke to the Ukrainian delegation and wrote an article about it. What struck her as a journalist in America was the fact that as the only accredited journalist from Ukraine, she was treated with special respect. Doors were opened for her everywhere. The people she was in contact with were polite and friendly, and it was easy and pleasant to work with them. The Foreign Press Center's staff in New York and Washington DC sent her invitations to meetings, conferences, speeches of prominent politicians, and conventions. They asked her to write articles on Ukraine for American newspapers. Well-known American journalists sought advice, and foreign press agencies accredited in the United States asked her to comment on significant events in Ukraine.

Slava's life was filled with interesting meetings and creative work. She wrote many articles and sent them to the editor in Ukraine first by fax and later by e-mail. The readers liked her articles, according to the editor, with whom she constantly talked on the phone. In general Slava wrote about American life, which fascinated her more and more. She wrote as well about the Ukrainian community in America.

An article written about her, "The Only Accredited Correspondent of Ukraine to the United States," appeared in American-based Ukrainian newspapers that come out in America—*Freedom* and *Ukrainian News*. The famous Ukrainian-American writer and journalist Julian Movchan wrote, "Recently I looked through an interesting publication in English—The Foreign Correspondents in the United States, published by the Foreign Press Center in 1996. I found out from this release that almost every country is represented in the United States by not one, but a group of journalists; some of them were large numbers. For example, Greece was represented by 14 reporters; Germany, 193; Russia, 36; Poland, 16; Croatia, 8; Brazil, 54; and so on. While looking through the directory's pages, I was looking for Ukraine. On page 30, after the list of correspondents of Turkey, I saw the title "Ukraine," under which the inscription reads: "Slava Lysenko, Correspondent. *Youth of Ukraine*. Spring Glen, New York." It was obvious that Ukraine had only one correspondent accredited in the United State," stated Julian Movchan.

Slava visited many cities in America. Most of all she liked Washington DC—the intellectual center of the country, the honor and conscience of the nation. The control and management of the entire United States was concentrated here, not only for America but perhaps for the whole world. What struck her the most was the correct classical architecture of low buildings in the baroque style in the city center, the vast quiet streets, wide sidewalks for pedestrians, and the large, carefully arranged parks.

Washington was not like any other city in America. It had a particularly great, solemn look. The office buildings on Constitution

Avenue in general seemed like museums. It seemed that a particular community lives here. And indeed, ordinary Americans, most of whom were of African origin, worked there. In Washington, this ethnic group took precedence over all others and was as much as 68 percent of the multinational population of the US capital. Slava had to talk in Washington mostly to people of African-American origin. She liked them for their kindness and sincerity, easy communication, and compassion for others' problems. There was something naturally human in these people that other peoples had lost by adapting and settling in this highly developed civilization.

Traveling through America, Slava would return as soon as possible to Spring Glen to see the teacher again, to share her experiences with him and hear his wise stories… Later on she felt telepathically connected with the teacher's thoughts while she was away from him on a business trip. He gave her wise advice on how to behave in a foreign country; he was interested in her journalism work. Slava helped the teacher edit a book on which he had worked for the past few years. Then she read proofs to him of his new book. The teacher was seventy-six years old, and it was difficult for him to read texts in small print. His eyes over the years were not very well, and he needed help. And Slava was the only person who was there and could help him type letters and his books. She read the letters he received from around the world, many from Ukraine. He tried to answer almost every letter, and not one was left unattended. Ukrainian Native believers from Ukraine asked him to send them his books and turned to him for help in the implementation of the ancient ancestors' ceremonies. The teacher decided to publish his book in Ukraine, in which he gave answers to hundreds of questions that people had asked in letters to him.

The editor of the newspaper *Youth of Ukraine* proposed Slava to record the teacher's interviews and answer some questions from the readers of the newspaper. It was a very interesting plan. Only few knew about spiritual teacher, and his science about Native Faith was inaccessible to people because of the absence of his books in Ukraine (the teacher's books were printed in the United States and Canada). Thus began the acquaintance of readers with the Ukrainian spiritual teacher (he was a spiritual guru for Ukrainian Native believers, similar to the Dalai Lama for Buddhists). She conveyed his thoughts in very accessible form so that the reader unprepared to accept new knowledge could understand simple human truth: Who am I? Why do I live? Who are my ancestors? Do I know the true history of my country? What was the culture and faith in Kievan Rus before Christianity was adopted? Why did Prince Volodymyr (Vladimir) forcibly baptize the Kievan Rus?...

When Slava prepared interviews with the teacher, she gathered a lot of stories written by him that had not been published elsewhere. She decided to write a book about the teacher, his family tree, his life, and his faith in Dazhboh (the ancient name of the god in Kievan Rus). A year later the book was written and published in Ukraine. This monograph went into details of the teacher's life and spiritual work. In this book were magnified the ideals of freedom and spiritual independence, love, great humanism—concepts that were as holy to the author as they were to every free person on planet Earth.

The Slava's articles about spiritual teacher and interviews with him were published in many newspapers in Ukraine, United States, England, and Australia. Here is the interview "Questions and Answers" which was published in Ukrainian-American newspapers.

Question (Slava): People who preach your spiritual knowledge call you the Spiritual Teacher. What is your concept of God Dazhboh?

Answer (Teacher): Dazhboh is the Consciousness of the world.
Dazhboh,
You are the Holy Spirit of my people,
You are One, I worship only You.
You are Almighty, my faith in You is almighty,
You are Eternal, my people are eternal.
Dazhboh,
I love You, that love will exist in my people,
I worship You, that my people have native faith.
I defend You, that my people have Liberty,
Glory to You!

Question: Idealists believe that Idea (Spirit) is the Primary Substance of the world. They call it God. Materialists believe that Matter is the Primary Substance of the world. They are atheists. If Dazhboh is the Consciousness of the world, then what is your conception of Consciousness? Do you have a new trend in philosophy, a new form of faith in God?

Answer: Traditionally these are question for philosophy. But philosophy today is dead, and Professor Stephen Hawking of the

University of Cambridge openly said about this. Philosophy has not kept up with modern development of humanity. To understand the universe at the deepest level, we need to know not only how the universe behaves, but why. And answer to this question we can find in Vedas, the man's oldest spiritual books. At the end of the 20th century people got access to the Vedas, whish contained in-depth knowledge about universe, about nature and history of mankind on Earth in the past few hundred thousand years; they also contained predictions of future events which were vainly ignored by modern science.

My conception of God is the modern interpretation of spiritual knowledge of the Vedas. I believe Dazhboh is the Primary Substance – all-embracing Consciousness of the world. (In Vedas Dazhboh means: dazh, da – to give, and boh, bhu – existence; these words are taken from Sanskrit language). Consciousness of the world is light, action, energy, will, eternity, infinity, gravitation… Consciousness of the human cannot exist without the Consciousness of the world.

Question: Then what is Spirit and Matter?

Answer: Spirit and Matter are children of Dazhboh, twins in whom are different peculiarities of Consciousness of the world, and their own original ramification.

Spirit is the substance of will and action, part of the consciousness of the Creator. Matter (atom) is a microstructure of energy. Energy is in light and light is in energy. Spirit and Matter are kindred of light, eternity and infinity.

Light is in life and life is in light. Nonlife and life always are calling on one another. The not living neuron and the living (natural) neuron react to one another.

In the history of science people have discovered a sequence of better and better theories, from Plato to the classical theory of Newton to modern quantum theories. But quantum and classical physics are based on different conceptions of physical reality.

Professor Isaac Asimov of Boston University, an American author, best known for his works of science fiction, wrote the novel "The Gods Themselves" in which he described the story about an unknown chemist who in the year 2070 accidentally stumbles upon the greatest discovery of all time, the electron pump, which produces unlimited energy for free… After this discovery he was hailed as the greatest scientist of all time. The company he forms becomes one of the richest corporations on the planet, putting the oil, gas, coal, and nuclear industries out of business. Where is all this energy coming from? Eventually the author Asimov uncovers the secret… This energy is pouring in from a hole in space connecting our universe to a parallel universe, and the sudden influx of energy into our universe is setting off a chain reaction that could eventually destroy the stars and even galaxies, turning the sun into a supernova, and destroying the Earth with it…

Now, the question is: Is it possible to extract energy from nothing? Yes, it is. Everything is possible in this world. Scientists have only recently realized that the "nothing" of the vacuum is not empty at all, but teaming with activity… Nikola Tesla, a genius of the twentieth century, Serbian-born physicist, was the first proponent of zero-point energy, that is, the idea that vacuum may possess unlimited quantities of energy. Tesla believed that he could extract unlimited energy from the vacuum, and he proved this. But humanity was not ready for this discovery at that time. It is a fundamental low of the universe: nothing becomes something, and something becomes nothing... And Tesla knew about this.

Question: Is the world the motion, the changes, disappearance and appearance of phenomena?

Answer: So, it is. Every second planets perish and every second new planets appear. Every second stars are extinguished and every second new stars appear. Every second ten million erythrocytes die in the body of a man and every second the same number (no more, no less) is born...

Galaxies in the universe are born from the primary matter (ether), and after the cycle of development die, again giving the birth to new galaxies, as is done with grass or leaves of trees throughout the year... In other words, the universe is the fluctuation of matter in space and time, and the universe is always there. The development cycle of our galaxy is described in detail in "Book of Wisdom" (one of the books of Vedas).

The world is an eternal change of forms and contents. And one day in the distant future humanity will have the last day on Earth. Eventually, billions of years from now, the sky will be on fire. The Earth will die in flames as it is consumed by the sun...

Probably five billions from now both the sun and the Milky Way galaxy will perish: the sun will mutate into a gigantic red star, and Milky Way galaxy will collide with the neighboring Andromeda galaxy. The Vedas predicted how the world will end in the event of a natural catastrophe. However, one day people must leave the Earth or die.

On a scale of millennia, one danger to human civilization is the emergence of a new ice age. The last ice age ended 10,000 years ago, when the next one arrives 10,000 to 20,000 years from now. Mankind has flourished within the recent tiny interglacial period, when the Earth has been unusually warm, but such a cycle cannot last forever… Life on Earth is so precious, that human should spread to at least one other inhabitable planet in case of a catastrophe… Vedas tell us that people appeared on Earth by the migration on the large spacecraft Vaitmar (each Vaitmar could carry up 144 Vaitmans, extraterrestrial human moved large distances of planetary scale by means of Vaitmans and between planets by means of Vaitmars). And on Earth at that time were only plants and animals, but monkeys are not yet evolved to the level of intelligent beings, what are the people.

Some of star immigrants came to the Earth because their planets at that time no longer existed –were destroyed by dark forces or disappeared in the event of a natural catastrophe. Given that humanity must one day flee the solar system to the nearby stars to survive, or perish, the question is: how will they get there? The nearest star system, Alpha Centauri, is over 4 light-years away, and modern rockets barely reach 40,000 miles per hour: at that speed it would take 70,000 years just to visit the nearest star… So, I give advice to read the unique manuscripts Vedas, and find there the answer to this question. Our ancestors had more accurate information not only about the galaxy or our solar system (they new its history and structure) but also how to design starships. Our ancestors knew that our galaxy Milky Way contains about 200 billion stars which are grouped into four curved arms – swasthya.

(The word swasthya or swastika came from the Sanskrit, meaning "well-being", "happiness", "good luck", this is the sign designating the galaxy Milky Way.) We can see the galaxy edge on summer nights: our solar system is located in the Orion arm close to the periphery of the galaxy Milky Way. Therefore, our observations of galactic arms even with telescopes are virtually inaccessible, and modern scientists find only two of them.

Question: Teacher, and what about the Mayan calendar?

Answer: There is no end to life, to intellect and the perfection of humanity. Its progress is everlasting. The Mayans never predicted the end of the world, on the contrary, they predicted rebirth of our planet. Their calendar described the end of the old cycle of eras. The Mayan calendar began with the fifth great cycle in 3114 B.C. and could end on 21 December 2012 A.D.

The Night of Svarog (in Sanscrit: Kali-Uga, one of the four stages of development that the world goes through as part of the cycle of eras) began about 3,600 years ago and could end in summer 2012 A.D. The Night of Svarog, according to the Vedas, is the name of a dark difficult time when our solar system passes through spaces of the dark worlds. The Golden Age, the age of truth and enlightenment (in Sanscrit: Sati-Uga) could easily begin in 2012. Earth's entry into the Golden Age is a time of transition from life as we have known it into life totally in harmony with Nature. The Golden Age will last for 10,000 years from now.

Question: Teacher, the global changes are coming on the Earth?

Answer: Absolutely. We are in process of making real practical changes that will support this next cycle of global consciousness.

In order for a new humanity to birth, then the structures of the old humanity need to be dismantled and transformed to make way for the new...

Everything in the universe is energy vibrating at one frequency or another, and when Earth was in prime health all of her life forms were vibrating harmoniously. Now Earth is crying for us to awaken our hearts to her heart, so we can move forward united in this new cycle. When we neglect our Mother Earth – destroy her clean waterways, clear forest, spew pollution into our air - we are hurting our selves and future generations to come.

Mother Earth is speaking to us and awakening us in the only way she knows how through the movement of her elements – Earth (earthquakes, volcanoes), Fire (bush fires), Water (floods, tsunamis), Air (hurricanes or cyclones). People have the power to work with the cycles of Mother Earth and make transition peacefully into a new age... we just need to listen and breath with our hearts not our egos.

Question: Teacher, what is your prediction of the future?

Answer: In the nearest future our extraterrestrial brothers once again begin to visit families of the Great Race on the planet Earth. They use Star Gates that are power complexes, which utilize gravitational and space-time spins or torsion systems that are used for moving between planets and star systems. They will help people to master new technologies and give them knowledge on the development of spirituality necessary for them at that moment. And one day it will be possible to build starships that can travel faster than the speed of light, to read other people's minds (telepathy), to move objects with power of our mind or even operate machines by power of our mind, to become invisible, to walk through walls, to transport our bodies instantly through outer space... When we bring science and spirituality together, we have the power to transform our planet into a positive future beyond the limits of our third dimensional experiences...

What we will see more on the planet is crashing of financial system, the coming to justice of those who abuse their places of power... We are going to experience more of the movements in Earth and her elements if we do not fully embrace the changes that need to take place on the planet to support the anchoring of higher dimensional frequency in the physical body as we enter to the Golden Age. A new world will not be a world based of materialism but it will be based of spirituality.

Question: Why the world is a world in which we find ourselves?

Answer: The world is the world because Dazhboh-Creator creates a concord of contraries-harmony of interdependence between Spirit and Matter, which is eternal in its own changeable: conscious becomes unconscious and unconscious becomes conscious.

Question: Teacher, you stated that Dazhboh is light. Where does light come from?

Answer: Light comes from light. I believe: Dazhboh is light. Man is in light and light is in man, and therefore the substance of man is eternal, in it is will and action. Dazhboh is the Creator of all-creations.

Question: What is the meaning of the words "Dazhboh – Creator of all-creations"?

Answer: I just explained: matter (atom) is a microstructure of energy. Dazhboh is an all-embracing Consciousness of the world that is light, action, will, eternity, infinity, gravitation... If there were no Dazhboh-Creator, an atom would cease to be an atom and extinction of the sun and stars would begin. The cosmos would change into a cemetery, peculiarities and forms which the human brain will never be capable of imagining...

The life-giving balance in solar system, where people of the planet Earth live, is harmonized by Dazhboh-Consciousness, in which is the will of eternal action that is energy.

Question: Do you preach the knowledge of God? Did God reveal his knowledge to you?

Answer: I preach the knowledge about God, his name is Dazhboh. According to the Vedas: Aryans, Slavs (Slavic people, descendants of Aryans, are present-day Ukrainians, Belarusians, Russians, Poles, Slovaks, Czechs, Bulgarian, Serbians, Croatians, Slovenes and Macedonian), Rusychi (Latin language: Ruthenians, people of Ruthenia, the Slavic-Aryan empire in the time of great antiquity, also known as Great Tartary) were descendants of the Heavenly Clan and sons or grandsons of Dazhboh (Dazdbog).

The Heavenly Clan are representatives of the developed civilizations, they created a Great Race; in ancient times people and heavenly gods (they came to our planet on the aircraft Wightman over 40,000 years ago) fraternized among themselves, and heavenly gods left to their terrestrial brothers and sisters and descendants their wise precepts. Dazhboh gave nine books containing sacred Vedas to representatives of the Great Race. Ancestral home of our ancestors

(Atlantis, Aryans and Slavs) was the solar system of Golden Sun (Dazhboh Sun), modern name – Beta Lion, Denebola.

The representatives of the Heavenly Clan were first who settled in the Midhard Earth (the ancient name of our planet), according to the Vedas. Ancestors of the terrestrial mankind came to planet Earth from various star systems at different times and they have different skin color: the Great Race – white, the Great Dragon – yellow, the Fiery Serpent – red, and representatives of star systems of the Gloomy Heath land – black.

The knowledge about God and the knowledge of God are two different comprehensions. Man created knowledge about God.

The level of knowledge about God depends on the level of spiritual and mental development of man. God is absolute, and the knowledge of absolute knows absolute only…

Question: Is faith born there, where man is?

Answer: Evidently. Animals have no faith. The will (inspiration willing) is born by the action of Dazhboh. A man is born, thus the volition is born to believe, to hope, to love, to live.

Faith is born where there is inspired volition to divinize light, beauty, charity, love, power, courage, mentality. From these sources arise faith in God…

Question: Is Dazhboh he or she?

Answer: Dazhboh is the consciousness of the world. The world is in consciousness and consciousness is in the world.

Dazhboh as a father manifests himself in the masculine gender. And Dazhboh as a mother manifests herself in the feminine gender. The Lord our Dazhboh exists everywhere.

Question: Can an icon be painted of Dazhboh?

Answer: No. The image of Dazhboh is the world-created consciousness. The image of Dazhboh is the action of eternity and infinity. Man has a limited imagination. Limited cannot imagine unlimited. Do you want to see Dazhboh in order to believe that he exists? Well… Brain-wave exists? Yes… Look!

Question: Teacher, conviction exists that there is only one truth…?

Answer: Yes, there is one truth. But in the world more than one definition of truth dominates. And therefore: truthful is not truthful, not truthful is truthful. Holy is not holy, not holy is holy; strong is weak and weak is strong…

Subjective truth is objective truth, objective truth is subjective truth. Definition of absolute truth and definition of relative truth is necessary. They stimulate the volition to perfect norms of concepts.

There exists a philosophy of peace loving truth, and exists a philosophy of violent truth. A nation has the right to have its own philosophy of truth. But also a nation has no the right to establish it by force in the land of another nation.

In the native philosophy of truth every nation in the course of the centuries embodies ideals of their own spirit, their own original pathway of life. Ukrainian people as well as other Slavic nations in ancient time lived on norms of life based on the millennial wisdom of Slavic-Aryan Vedas. According to these norms they, descendants of the Heavenly Clan (Rod) and the grandsons of their God – Dazhboh – could not accept the dogmas of alien religion Christianity that transformed all Slavic people into slaves of alien God.

And the morality is one. But many different definitions of morality exist. What is moral for the Indian is immoral for the Japanese, and what is moral for the Japanese is immoral for the Indian.

Different definitions of truth or morality are not immoral. They are created by different characteristics of nations and the different pathways of their spiritual development.

Question: Teacher, as I understand there are many concepts, many definitions of God?

Answer: Yes. God is one. There are many religions because there are many different concepts of God. An Indian says Brahma, a Persian says Agura Mazda, and a Jew says Adonai, Sabaot, and an Arab says Allah, a Greek says Zeus, and a Ukrainian says Dazhboh… An Arab having the knowledge of Muhammad believes that the Arabian concept of God Allah is truthful. And he, for instance, does not need Japanese concept of Deity (Amaterasu Omikami). Japanese faith is Japanese spiritual originality in which are developed peculiarities of Japanese character, the pathway of Japanese life and its moral basis. There is a native land and there is a strange land. There is a native concept of God and there is a strange concept of God.

Different concept of God should not provoke hostility among men. The differences in the concepts of God enrich the spiritual life of mankind.

Question: Do you preach religious tolerance?

Answer: There is only humanity and the grace of God, where the believers of one faith have tolerant attitudes to the believers of the other faiths. Blessed art thou, Dazhboh!

Question: Teacher, my brother joined a religion sect as it promised to give him eternity and to free him from sins. What do you think about this?

Answer: Behind you is eternity and before you is eternity. You are born and you live in eternity, the name of it is the world. Sin exists there, where violence in feelings, thoughts and the body exists. A Hell or I named it as a space of dark energies is in the soul of a man who weakens his mind with own sins and negative thoughts.

Sins exhaust a soul by disturbances; sins cloud the pathway of thoughts and oppress the positive energy of life. Man must free himself from sins, doing good things for himself and people and thinking positively. He, who frees you from sins, strengthens his dominance on your soul. Be the lord of your own ego.

Question: There are believers who live in fear. They are afraid of God's punishment and they are afraid of the temping devil. They are suffering from fear. Teacher, can you advise these people?

Answer: God is love. We live in his love and his love lives in us. Do not be afraid to believe in love, glorify love. Love is the prayer of the soul, the great treasure of Heaven and Earth. Love is the spiritual joy: were there is joy there is health, inspiration and desire to live and work with pleasure. Love is happiness, which is necessary for you and other people. The purpose of faith is for the perfection of the humanity, not for fear…

The devil is evil, a negative creature of this world. It is necessary to fight evil. Be afraid to be a friend of the devil. From goodness arises goodness; from evil arises evil. Positive thinking and positive feeling are divine cure of illnesses and fears. I recommend a meditation. To the important purpose of prayer belong complacence, control tension and worry, equilibrium and inspired energy of human, quietness of mind and self-harmony with faith in God.

Question: Teacher, you told that the human is of extraterrestrial origin according to the Vedas. Who is the man? What is the nature of reality?

Answer: The universe where human live now, is closed on itself in a "wheel of life". Imagine that you have a special microscope, and you begin to look into a drop of blood. First, you would see living cells, then molecules, atoms, electrons and other smaller pieces, and then you would be able to see entities that are the souls, then what we call spirit and the spirit is our universe, whish consists of galaxies that consist of star systems, planets, beings, bodies, organs and cells. Finally we come to from where we started...

Everything in the universe consists of a set of energies. The distribution of energy has created a great spirits - the ultimate beings, parts of the Dazhboh-Creator. One of such spirits planed to create a new world inside itself. The other ultimate spirits that were smaller decided to help him in that creation becoming a part of it. Together, they have created spaces of Prav, Nav and Yav (substances of Dazhboh-Creator) which differed from each other by frequencies, the upper space penetrated into the lower, but not vice versa.

To continually gain strength, the great spirit has established the flow of spirits inside yourself through the more dense worlds of Nav and Yav, and back to yourself in Prav. Thus, spirits created in the spaces new worlds, embodying themselves in them, creating a special energy, that fueled the great spirit, and expanded its boundaries.

The Creator created the stars and planets, and great spirits helped him to combine all of them into galaxies. The Creator created the soul and the different bodies, to embody his spirit parts in the created universe on various planets. So there were created new life forms inside the body of the Creator. And this cycle is everlasting.

Yav is the world we all know. We know it better than all others, because our minds set on it since birth. This is the densest of all worlds – a world of gross matter, the world of third dimension. Thanks to the world Yav you body can get enormous power, fueling the other bodies, soul and spirit. Of course, if we keep our body in good health.

The Nav space is filled with several worlds. Modern people have given the names of these worlds – ethereal, astral and mental, though these names do not accurately describe worlds themselves. Ethereal world often is referred to "mirror", as the dense world is reflected in it, as in the water. It is a kind of tight world, very similar to our Yav world. And human beings inhabit it. They can see us from their world, which also has plants and other life forms, similar to our world, but eating one another is missing. Some civilizations have continued its chronicle of the earth in the ethereal world and still live there.

The astral world is created just so that the soul has the opportunity to live situations that could never happen in our Yav world. In it, as in the dense world, there are trees and a variety of creatures. This world consists of two worlds – the second world, as the first is a superstructure. Everyone is out there in a dream. This is the most driven of all possible worlds that we know.

In the astral world everything goes according to script, without the right to choice for the creatures that inhabit it: they are a figment of the imagination, but still alive. Some creatures of the astral world can share their power, and some - take it out. This world allow to human live many lives in one, adding to the affairs of the dense world astral things. Astral world it would be better described as fabulous or the world of dream...

The mental world is different. It is divided into dolls in the likeness of the world – one in the other. Fruits for food are not provided there – all the energy feed only. The main food of this world is the energy of the stars, and vegetation in this world is only ocean energy, and substance is different, but still reasonable.

The creatures of this world have more freedom, than we do. But the power of the mind of man in this world is as a man-god, enclosed in a dense body. Mental world provides the world of constructions. It was originally created by various creatures and filling by energies despise being new to the lowest worlds. I would call this world - creative.

All these worlds are tied to the planets, as living entities, and they are the total volume of Nav.

There is also the Slav space between the worlds. In this space the souls live. Borders of Slav, Nav and Prav are touched. In the Slav space there is sub world – its name is purgatory. Souls get there after incarnations to cleanse the energies of the heavy, nasty, obtained in the incarnation. If the soul filled with the energy that is a poison for the spirit, this contaminated part of the soul will be disassembled by nodes and that action is painful... If the energy that filled the soul after the incarnation is clean, it will pass through purgatory.

When the soul is filled with high quality (high frequencies) realization of the subtle energies the spirit can pick them up and go to the Prav, its home, receiving a huge force. It means that the spirit has fulfilled its purpose, having raised a notch in the genus. The empty matrix of the soul will be used by other spirit. But if it's time for spirit to return to Prav and it not collected the necessary energy, then the soul goes to the spirit in the upper purgatory, between the Slav space and the Prav, were the subtle energies of the spirit is selected and then spirit divides. One piece, that is lighter, goes to Prav, and another that is heavier with the soul goes back to the Slav for future incarnations.

Space of Prav is a place of clean spirits. To fill the power they go for a journey from Prav into the worlds of dense. To do this, there were created souls and different bodies.

When spirit gains the necessary strength, it returns back into the Prav and begins to create new life and new worlds, new planets, new stars, even galaxies..., expanding the space of Prav and universe itself. It means that our spirit is able to go to the world of law - Prav, and there will continue to develop without the soul, the shells and bodies, and if necessary to create for itself a body, soul, and sheath, and manifest itself in some form of new life or new world...

Now, let consider who the man is. To have ability of developing in new worlds for the particles of the spirit of the Creator, he (Dazhboh) created a soul – the special live device that collects unique experience. This experience is the energy that nourishes and strengthens the spirit.

To bring the soul into one of the worlds, many different bodies were created by the great spirits, which are parts of the Creator. To embody the soul in a human, it requires 4 bodies – mental, astral, etheric and dense. These bodies are temporary, they are created for a single embodiment, but at the same time they help the soul to evolve in 4 worlds.

The dense body is linked with the thinner bodies by chakras, through which energy flows, nourishing the body, soul and spirit. All four bodies with a soul linked with a special shell that unites the entire structure into human being. Thus, the human is born in one of the worlds of Yav or Nav, starting a new life, gaining experience and impressions of his creation. That experience is a memory that stores in bodies, soul and spirit.

A human can recall the essence of all past incarnations if his lifestyle is wise. But not all life events saved in a soul, but only a special, new – without repetition. Energy, which soul received from life experiences, essentially is different in quality. A being will reincarnate until its soul gain quality power, locking its spirit. Only the constant development, creativity and righteous way of life will fill the soul with pure light and give food to the spirit and help him to return to his home, in Prav, with new knowledge and new strength.

Question: As I understand, each of us incarnated on Mother Earth for a particular purpose?

Answer: Yes, you are right. The human beings incarnated on this planet to improve themselves, to go through their life lessons, to get new experience, to gain quality power, and to fill their souls with clean energy, pure light... It is the same as a student does at the school. When a human completed all the homework, doing his lessons very well in this third dimensional world, his soul after reincarnation will go into the world with higher vibrations, starting a new life in Nav, as I just explained.

Anyone who does not succeed – has not fulfilled his lessons, will reincarnate again on this planet in another body; this process may occur many times – depending on the level of the development of a human's soul. For instance, an imperfect person cares about financial enrichment at the expense of others – he want to ease life for himself only by burdening the life of other people. Such person in the next life, after reincarnation, will be poor. It is his karma that this person has to improve himself in the next life doing good things for people. And there are beings of the Great Spirit that come to Earth from other worlds, planets to maintain the energy balance of our planet. They embody the soul in a human. They are children of Light; we call them – Indigo, Crystal children... Now the children of the Golden Sun are born on Earth. They come to teach people so that they go in the right direction of the development in harmony with the universe.

Every person who incarnated on Earth has some guardian spirit which we used to call guardian angels. There are spirits of different levels – from small (one of the spirit of our relatives) to the great spirit (our ancestor called Svarga, it means galaxy in which we live today; and the spirit being that control our galaxy is Svarog). Who is the guardian angel of the person – depends on his purpose. If the old soul or soul from the great spirit is embodied for a great task, then the spirits of mentors in humans will be powerful. If the soul is young the angels will be likely relatives – father or mother, grandmother or grandfather, or others.

Question: Teacher, what is the mission of guardian angels?

Answer: The task of the guardian angels to help you get out of the dark forces, take the path of destiny, the righteous way of life. They also protect you, control the flow of energy of your being, and open your abilities. Your life is directly linked to them. Your success is also their successes and your mistakes not only vitiate you soul, but their souls too. It is very important to establish contact with them, and then your teachers can greatly help you, and you accordingly – them. Angels take care of you whole life.

With a healthy way of thinking and living, a person can develop sensitivity and begin to hear their angelic mentors, as an inner voice or thought, or even in the form of images… But while such a link is not available, the guardian angels reveal themselves to human beings through the world of Yav – humans, animals, birds and a variety of circumstances…

Ask your guardian angels to give you a sign or hint in the difficult times of life and they always find a way to help you, and my advice is: keep the purity of body and soul, only then it will be easier to work with you. Over time, you will be able to go with them to communicate without intermediaries and together fulfill its mission to give the joy of accomplishment, happiness and wonderful life…

Question: Teacher, is there a guide how to live, a righteous way to find a true happiness, to improve yourself?

Answer: Of course. Our ancestors gave us unique books of wisdom – Vedas, which described the system of conceptions and norms of righteous living based on the millennial wisdom. In "Maha Vira" I wrote about seven laws of righteous way of life that based on the Vedic knowledge. They are:

1. Rightful thinking: freedom, purpose, courage.
2. Rightful volition: love, justice, consistency.
3. Rightful performance: responsibility, punctuality, discipline.
4. Rightful attitude towards yourself and your environment: independent ego, responsive ego, harmonious ego.
5. Rightful nourishment: natural food, ethnic food, customs.
6. Rightful love: hatred does not cease by hatred, hatred ceases by love; co-experience and devotedness; spiritual beauty and faithfulness, forgiveness.
7. Rightful faith: natural birth of faith, blissful understanding of faith, rightful aim of faith.

Detailed interpretation of seven Laws of righteous way of life is in "Maha Vira".

Human beings on Earth are imperfect creatures who can never wholly grasp perfection, but who are obligated to strive after it by the systematic improvements of their minds, the enrichment of their spiritual lives, diligent labour in vocations, and the improvement of their bodily health and fitness. We each exist for a short time on Earth, and in that time explore a small part of the whole universe.

I want to draw attention to a healthy way of thinking. The only thing that limits us is our thinking... Any poisonous substance or dark thoughts destroy our body structure, and the recovery takes a lot of forces. Love helps man to look with inspiration on life and the world. A man in love better understands himself, the people and the world. A man in love strives to improve himself. From love arise love and happiness.

If there be righteousness in the heart, there will be beauty in the character. If there be beauty in the character, there will be harmony in the home. If there be harmony in the home, there will be order in the nation...

This interview evokes a lively response from readers. The teacher received many letters and phone calls in response to the interview with him.

After the appearance in Ukraine of the magnificent book *Maha Vira,* the Native Faith movement began, issued chronologies, and created Native Faith communities. Such a phenomenon had never been in Ukraine before. The teacher had a huge internal energy, which woke up the Ukrainians (and not only Ukrainians) from the millennium's spiritual enslavement. For average Ukrainians it was difficult to understand that only people with a high sense of love could understand that it was time for awakening, a time to return to their home and holy sources. Nobody even thought that one man could do so much with his human life, that he could write such a magnificent book as *Maha Vira*. The teacher lighted the fireplace of a spiritual awakening on the planet.

Slava also visited Canada, to see how the native people were respected there. They are respectfully called First Nations. Slava went to see the opening of the winter Olympic Games in Vancouver, where guests from 147 countries were welcomed at the Olympic stadium by local tribes in their national dresses. In Canada, along with America, all national cultures and religions are honored. No one pursues anybody; it is a free, democratic country. What is important is that the local tribes even have a privileged status. They live separately in their settlements, cultivate their original culture and language, and practice their native beliefs. Their children have priority over others in being admitted to the universities, and their tuition is paid for by the state. When Slava compared the native Indian tribes with autochthonous Ukrainians, who profess the faith of their ancestors in Ukraine, she thought that the situation of Ukrainian native believers was extremely oppressed. These people were suffering persecution from the government officials. They tried to defame, demean, and slander the spiritual teacher. Slava wrote many different answers, and refutations of slanders and fabrications, about the teacher. Her articles were published in Ukrainian and American newspapers.

Slava remembered the snowy winter in New York State when through the long winter evenings she worked hard on the book, listening to incredibly interesting stories of the teacher with a cup of hot tea or some warm stewed fruit and pies she had baked herself. Sometimes she would get up in the morning and look out the window. There was as much as a meter of snow, making it impossible to go outside. Sometimes for several days the snow was not cleared from the roads in the mountains, as if time stood still. There were no cars and no people; only a sunny blue sky and white snow—a bewitching sight. It seemed that civilization stepped back for a moment, as if warning about its temporary nature in this world where the owner is Mother Nature, all powerful and overwhelming.

For the first time in her life Slava celebrated the ancient style of Christmas of the Sun by the Vedic calendar, which her ancestors had celebrated on December 24 at the winter solstice. The teacher gave Slava advice about how to prepare for the celebration and told her how to cook traditional Christmas dishes. Slava remembered that in Ukraine they had celebrated New Year's Eve on January 1 and the old style of New Year on January 13. The best memories of her childhood were associated with this celebration. Her mother cooked the most delicious dishes, including her favorite nut cake, and cakes with poppy seeds. On New Year's evening, a group of students from the college where her father worked used to come, wearing nice Ukrainian national dress. They came with music and sang old Ukrainian carols. Then her mother treated everybody to Christmas cookies, sweets, and cakes...

They were officially allowed to celebrate Christmas after Ukraine became independent. But Ukrainian families celebrated Christmas even during the Soviet times, although nobody said anything about it. People somewhere deep down felt that this event came from the ancestors, and the tradition was passed from generation to generation. They knew that the special celebration table should be set with twelve different dishes, including wheat porridge with honey, poppy seeds and nuts, which are called *kutya*, and stewed dried fruit (*uzvar*). On the table they put a clean bowl with a spoon for the ancestors, who, according to a popular belief, come at night to visit the *svyata vecherya* (holy supper). This act held the mystery of unity with the ancestors in an eternal family circle. The Didukh was honored with a sheaf of wheat as a symbol of new birth of the sun. When Christmas Eve came, the children came to sing carols and sprinkle your house with corn or wheat. The children had to be rewarded... It turns out that this tradition existed in Ukraine before the adoption of Christianity. Many people were not aware of these traditions.

Slava was wondering how folk celebrated Christmas in America. She could see everywhere—in large shops and offices, on the street in large and small squares—that people decorated Christmas trees. Everywhere near the houses and cottages there were bright, colorful scenes of illumination where you could see Santa Claus, who was brought to the New World by the first emigrants from Holland. Santa Claus was carrying gifts. It seems that the world around you for a short time was transformed into a Christmas fairy tale. In all stores and large malls from the first of December until the first day of January, modern Christmas tunes could be heard. The most popular among them was the world's most famous Ukrainian carol, "Shchedryk," known in the Western world as "Carol of the Bells" (a folk song written by the famous Ukrainian composer Mykola

Leontovych in the early twentieth century). This Ukrainian melody became popular abroad, and in 1936 Peter Vilhovskyy, who worked for NBC radio, wrote the English text to "Shchedryk." Today there are many remakes and instrumental variations of the melody.

In Slava's opinion this celebration doesn't have religious significance for most Americans and is more likely a secular celebration for them. Commercial shops are packed with Christmas goods, and people rush to buy everything they need for the celebration. They especially spend a lot of time shopping, looking for gifts. Americans love the Christmas holiday because they have almost a week at home and may spend some time with family. This is an American tradition—to celebrate Christmas and New Year's with gifts, lots of fun and games, and, as a rule, Santa Claus. The lifestyle of Americans is not religious; it is simply American, and a man is quite free in choosing his views of the world. Representatives of different nationalities and cultures live in America, and each ethnic group celebrates Christmas or New Year according to their traditions.

And how did our ancestors celebrate this day? How did it come to our modern world, and what does it mean?
Slava lay down a white-as-snow tablecloth on the table and put on it traditional twelve dishes: dumplings with cheese, dumplings with potatoes, cabbage rolls, fish, mushroom soup, pies with apples, sauerkraut with cranberry, salad with beetroots and prunes, wheat porridge with honey and nuts, *uzvar,* pastries with poppy seeds, and

a loaf round as the sun. The teacher blessed the holy supper; Slava said the prayer to Dazhboh:

"My Dazhboh, my lord, you are in a flower, an apple, and the blue skies of your infinity, in a rainbow's lights and in a poppy seed, and in the smile of a baby, the kindness of a mother, and in the faith of ancestors, who live in me today. Long live the holy mystery of love and beauty, infinity and eternity, my Dazhboh!"

The teacher's calm eyes looked at Slava for a moment and then he said:

"I believe: Dazhboh is light. I am in light and light is in me. There is no faith superior than Light. Dazhboh is truth. I am in truth and truth is in me. There is no faith superior than Truth. Dazhboh is love. I am in love and love is in me. There is no faith superior than Love. Dazhboh is eternity. I am in eternity and eternity is in me. There is no faith superior than Eternity. Dazhboh is my native God. I am in my God and dear God is in me. There is no faith superior than the native God… Our ancestors called the sun - God Dazhboh, in their imagination—the source of life on the planet Earth. They felt it by their enigma of its consciousness and unconsciousness.

"Christmas of light is celebration of living, celebration of light, celebration of ancestors, festival of freedom and happiness. We, Dazhboh's grandchildren, are meeting a Christmas of light by the holy supper, the holy thinking, and the holy soul unity. We are calling ritually our ancestors to come and join us for the holy supper because we have such a spiritual culture. Between them and us has always existed and will always be a natural and spiritual integrity.

The Christmas of light—the victory of light over darkness. It is the victory of good over evil, the victory of life over death. Humanity can't exist without Christmas of the Sun. The sun is not eternal: it may happen that an explosion in space quenches the sun. And our solar system will disappear. It may be that our planet, impaired by powerful explosions on the sun, flies into other solar systems. And there, finding a new sun, will begin a new life…

"This has not happened yet, just because the Christmas of Light (light of Dazhboh) each year acts as the life-giving force of Creator God in harmony with the forces of the solar system, with the forces of the near and far space worlds, and galaxies… In the space of the universe stars are constantly born and die, as well as solar systems and human civilizations. World—eternal change, eternal aging, and eternal youth…

"Our ancestors left us a warning—the Testament: People, come back to Mother Nature and reunite with her, and honor her. And remember: without Christmas (birth) of the Sun, humanity will perish. Today, to save human beings from degeneration on the planet Earth, we must teach them to love Mother Nature and the beauty encoded in its four symphonies (spring, summer, autumn, and winter). We must teach them to live in harmony with the surrounding universe. And we must remember: the first beliefs of this 5th civilization on the planet Earth appeared on the territory between the Carpathians and the Caucasus, to the north of the Black Sea.

"This original faith—faith in the God of sun—became the basis of a Vedic beliefs, the creators of which were our ancestors. The other different religions were created on the same basis, and with these religions came the desire to embody the sun in the owner, their ancestor, and to embody an ancestor in the sun (light—source of life). We know that in ancient Rome before the Christian era, people celebrated Christmas of God Mithra (*miter* means sun, and *God Mithra* means God of sun) on December 25 (the winter solstice birth of the sun). Mithra's pre-Christian roots are attested in the Vedic and Avestan texts, as well as by historian Herodotus.

"In almost all religions of the earth, Gods and sons of God, as the embodiment of light, salvation, victory of light over darkness, were born in winter to save people - to give them light, warmth, and the joy of new life. They are called Agni, Mithra (Mitra), Krishna, Adonis, Prometheus, Attic, Osiris, Tammuz, Buddha, and Jesus. The only difference is that they belonged to different nations and different ages.

"Man made religions replaced the first most natural birth of the Sun Festival… In almost all religions there is the same history of God's birth. Gautama Buddha was blamelessly born 500 years before the birth of Jesus. Savior Buddha descended from heaven in the bosom of the Virgin Maya to be a living god, the God Man, and to teach people how to be compassionate. The Egyptian goddess Izida (Isis) gave birth to a child named Horus. She was pursued by a cruel king, Set, and escaped with the child to the island Gemnos. Also Virgin Devaki in India with God's child Krishna escaped from King Kansa (1,200 years before the birth of Jesus). The Virgin Mary with Jesus, child of God, escaped to Egypt from King Herod... Sumerians brought to Babylon a faith in God Tammuz, who was born blamelessly.

"Christmas in all people is felt and understood in different ways, depending on their historical experience, spiritual development, and geographical location. And all of them believe that the light (holiness), which they embodied in the image of a man, was born blamelessly. From the world's first Christmas began Christmas celebrations in Europe and Asia, and they would be combined with the original Vedic ritual celebration Christmas of the Sun.

"We continue the traditions of our ancestors and celebrate the world's first Christmas, which they initiated: Christmas of the Sun. Our ancestors gave us the soul of their soul, the heart of their heart, an image of their image, the beauty of their beauty. And between their "I" and our "I" is the eternal sun ray of a hereditary power. Rejoice, human soul, the world of the powerful, majestic Christmas of Dazhboh Light is coming. Sun overcomes darkness, proclaims a new birth, a resurrection of life on Earth!"

The teacher folded his hands in a prayer and bowed. Slava also bowed in response.

The Christmas Eve ritual begins with a prayer and ends with a prayer of thanksgiving for the Dazhboh's gifts. The consumption of food begins with wheat kasha; the oldest in a family started tasting with a ceremonial bowl. You can help yourself to other dishes afterward. Our ancestors did not drink spirits, but they did drink stewed dried fruits and herbs.

It was the way they celebrated Christmas of the Sun.

In Ukraine many people now consider themselves Christians, and those traditions that came to them from the depths of centuries before the birth of Christ, they call Christian because they don't know it; they call their ancestors "savages," "believers in the sun." As proved by the evidence from historical and archaeological sources, all people's ancestors at one time were the most advanced people on Earth. They are the creators of the most ancient Vedic culture and civilization. The oldest calendar was recently found via excavation, and it was 12,000 years old. The year of this calendar was divided into four periods, 360 days. The ancient ancestors' faith is one of unity with nature, of a human soul's ability to feel and understand her. The instinct for self-preservation urged people to love nature and keep nature clean. Most existing religions have been cut off from nature and human happiness; they are guided by mysticism, and guided modern civilization in a way to distort the face of planet Earth. The civilization, which passes a sentence to nature, is doomed to destruction. The law of nature guides everything that lives on planet Earth. Where nature is sick, the soul and body is sick. Mother Nature is patient, but only for the time being. That is why humanity has to become fit, to return to its roots, to revive the spiritual unity with the ancestors who lived in harmony with nature. This age of human self-destruction will end. According to the oldest spiritual books of humanity, Vedas, the new era of light is coming.

Asylum

The time of tireless creative work and stability of life in America changed for Slava to a time of severe trial for her and all of her family. She was forced to become a political refugee. Slava did not expect that her articles and books published in Ukraine would be labeled by some Russian journals as "American propaganda." It was a time in Ukraine when the pro-Communist majority was in Parliament and people with Soviet mentality ruled the country. They looked at the world through the glasses of the past and continued to spread propaganda as an old habit. One piece of this propaganda said that America gave asylum to Ukrainian nationalists, and America wanted to rule the world. For this purpose, they spread this propaganda in former Soviet countries to set their expansion there. Anyone who was a fan of the Western orientation of democratic development of the country they called nationalists, American spies… This ruling elite feared the manifestations of freedom, the truth about the historical past of Ukraine, even all that regarded the American way of life as positive. To add to this unfavorable attitude was the opinion of some religious figures—it will be correct to say religious fanatics—who criticized Slava's articles about the teacher, the ancient philosophy of the ancestors, which she published in *Youth of Ukraine* and in her book about him. We know that in Ukraine only one religion is considered privileged: the Orthodox Greek rite is under the jurisdiction of the Moscow Patriarchate (the majority church in Ukraine – the one under the Moscow Patriarchate – called the Ukrainian Orthodox Church). Other religions in Ukraine were considered atypical and experienced pressure from the authorities.

Volodymyr Bodenchuk, the editor in chief, wrote a letter to Slava and forwarded some newspapers that contained her articles. He wrote in his letter that there was furious pressure from above not to publish any more of her articles. He also sent her clippings from the newspapers *Izvestia* and *Kiev News,* in which were printed a spiteful article about her that humiliated her honor and reputation, unjustly accusing her of writing articles about America because she was "well paid for it."

Also, her father wrote a letter from Kiev, in which he told her that he had received threats and intimidation over the phone and from an unknown man who met him on the street when he came home from work. Her dad wrote that the man spoke inappropriate language, threatened him, and told him that his daughter had to stop her journalistic work and never write articles and books. He followed her father and shouted that his nest would be destroyed if she did not stop the American propaganda. Then he abruptly pushed her father in the shoulder, nearly knocking him down before he disappeared, as if he were not there. Slava's dad wrote that this was the first time in his life someone had acted so brutally toward him.

After that incident he went to work and always looked around to see if he was being followed.

Slava spoke with her mother and daughter on the phone: they were scared. After being pushed in the shoulder by the unknown assailant, her father suffered from back pain, and it took a long time for him to recover. Her mother said that they were afraid to go out alone and that her daughter, Lelya, was not allowed anywhere on her own. Slava's mother even accompanied her to and from school.

Slava telephoned her relatives in Kiev every day. She was constantly worried about them. When she talked on the phone, she would hear a strange noise—a noise that arose during a conversation that made it difficult to hear. Some strange things happened, and it was a mystery. There was not anyone to turn to and complain and from whom she could seek help; it seemed that everything in her native Kiev conspired against her and her family.

Later on, her father wrote another letter (he could not talk about it on the phone, because their phone was bugged). Her father said that a man who called himself Colonel Ignatenko came to his place of employment and made inquiries about his daughter. He wanted to know the means by which Slava had published a book in Kiev, and who had paid her for the article printed in the Ukrainian newspapers. He also said it would be better for her if she stopped writing favorable articles and books about America. In his letter her father pleaded with her not to write and not to publish any articles in Ukraine, because it threatened the entire family.

It was sad and painful to read such letters. Slava further felt the divide between her two worlds: the world where she was now living, where she could freely express her opinions, no one intended to intimidate her, and she was a free person; and the world where her family was living in fear each day, where you could hear a threat to innocent people, where there were all sorts of restrictions, where there was no freedom of choice, the human being was defenseless, and one's human rights and freedoms were breached…

Slava asked herself why there was such a hopeless situation in Ukraine. Why couldn't they destroy the Communist slave stereotypes? Those who wanted to do it, even in the way Slava had tried through the honor of her journalistic activities, became objectionable to that young post-Soviet country. It was in the initial stages of democratic development, but still all bureaucratic, with a number of prohibitions and restrictions on society. The Soviet Union had collapsed, but former officials still worked there, and their ambitions had turned into the instinct to prohibit, control, and restrict freedom even in its smallest manifestation.

Fear breeds fear, and in a society where the government keeps people in fear, that same government is afraid of the manifestations of freedom, free thinking, and the best traditions of democracy. Many journalists and writers who sympathized with the democratic West, who wrote the truth about the Holodomor, the tragic Ukrainian past, the victims of Soviet totalitarianism, the limitation of rights and freedoms of Ukrainian citizens, about lawlessness and corruption, fell onto the "black" list of "unreliable": they were followed, their articles were not printed, they were persecuted, and worse. In ten years of independence, thirty-seven journalists were killed in Ukraine.

Slava turned to her sponsor and a good friend Ray Lapika to seek qualified legal advice (he was the president of the law firm Lapika Law Corporation). A week later she received a letter and application forms from Lapika that he told her to complete and send to Immigration Services of the United States. There were application forms to seek political asylum. Lapika advised Slava in his letter to seek political asylum in the United States as the only way to be protected from persecution in Ukraine. He also warned her that it would not be so easy for her or for her family who remained in Kiev. To pass these tests, she needed to be strong and patient, because it required a great responsibility and a sustained belief that you were doing everything right. Then in a letter he wrote: "It is difficult to prove to the US government your right to obtain refugee status. To become a political refugee, you will need to show your well-founded fear of persecution in Ukraine because of your race, religion, nationality, political opinion, or membership in a particular social group. In other words you should prove that you will be subject to torture, that your life will be at risk, or that you risk cruel treatment or punishment. You have to prove you cannot get protection in your country. You should think twice before taking these drastic steps, because it will forever change your life. Only strong people can decide on it. And God help you, I hope that fate is favorable to you and you are granted the status of a political refugee in America. Only then can you start a new life and feel like you are truly a free person. So do not waste time. Fill out the application for this process of gaining political refugee status. Asylum could take you two to three years. If you need my help, just call me. Enclosed is the supporting letter to US Citizenship and Immigration Services to provide you the status of political asylum. You should send it along with the application. I wish you good luck. Sincerely, Ray."

Slava talked to many journalists from other countries. She became a member of the International Women's Media Foundation. In Washington Slava attended a press conference organized by this group for a journalist from Iran, Suleima Afshar; she was granted political asylum in the United States because of her persecution at home. Slava talked with her and asked questions about how she had arrived in the United States and received status as a political emigrant. The reporter, Suleima Afshar, willingly shared her experience in obtaining political asylum and advised Slava to ask for help from Freedom House and Georgetown University. The students of the Georgetown University Law School, which has a legal clinic, had helped her complete the applications and documents for submission to US Immigration Services.

Also at this press conference Slava met Nadia, a journalist from the Voice of America Ukrainian Service, who had come from Ukraine to the United States and married an American. She willingly shared her stories about her immigrant life and how she met her husband while working as a guide for foreign tourists in Kiev. Nadia invited Slava to visit their publishing office in Washington, DC, on Independence Avenue. On the same day after the press conference she offered to bring Slava to her house in the suburb of Silver Spring, Maryland. Slava was interested to see how immigrants from Ukraine settle, and she agreed. Nadia had her car, which she had learned to drive when she came to America. In the evening they came to a nice new two-story house where Nadia lived. The house was empty; Nadia's husband was on a business trip. Nadia prepared a delicious dinner and lighted a fire in the fireplace. It was very comfortable in the spacious, modern, furnished apartment.

After so many tense and anxious days, Slava for the first time felt the tiredness leave her body. She was pleased to spend time in the company of her new friend, and felt the pleasure of communication and Ukrainian hospitality, and the comfort of home warmth from a friendly hostess.

Slava told Nadia about herself and about her journalistic experience in America, and about the intimidation and persecution of her family in Ukraine.

Nadia supported Slava's decision to seek political asylum in the United States. She sympathized with Slava, offered to help her, and wanted her to be granted legal immigration status in America. Nadia advised Slava to move from New York to Washington, DC, and offered to let her stay in her house during this time. She said, "You have to be here, in Washington, in the center of all events, not in Spring Glen's mountains. All of us will help you. You can't imagine how long it takes and how difficult a process it is to be granted asylum in this country. Your address is known to everybody. Probably they already know where you live, and I saw it myself in the address book in the Foreign Press Center. Tomorrow is Saturday and I have a day off. We can go to Spring Glen by my car tomorrow to collect your stuff and come back on Sunday. Do you like this idea?"

Slava was happy with the idea; she didn't know how to be grateful to this generous woman. Now she was completely convinced that she was making the right choice: she was going to seek asylum in the USA. She was happy to meet such beautiful people who would be there for her in a difficult time. She had to follow her fate and go toward her future…

Nadia showed her a room on the first floor where Slava could live. It was a small, cozy room, the window of which looked out to the garden behind the house. Slava immediately liked her new place of residence. Without hesitation she agreed to temporarily live at Nadia's house until her immigration case could be sorted out. Nadia didn't ask for a payment, just said, smiling, "When you get legal status to stay in America, find work, then find a better home, I'll come and visit you and we'll have a cup of coffee together."

In the morning two journalists went to New York State. Both of them originally came from Ukraine, and each had her own destiny. For one of them everything in her life was simple, without much difficulty: she had married a wealthy American, studied at the prestigious Georgetown University in Washington, DC, gotten a job at the National Broadcasting Company (NBC), and worked for the Voice of America as a journalist. The other had a life full of severe trials and persecution, threats, ups and downs—everything a person had to know about the real nature of this life. Indeed, she had to suffer, and pass rigorous tests in life, and that was not her fault. A person by nature is born free, and becoming an adult means always fighting for that right given by nature. Slava perceived the world with certain sensitivity. She saw something others did not see. She saw herself in a different world—a perfect world, which she was looking for in this very different and imperfect world.

In the evening they arrived in Spring Glen. It was February, and in the Catskill Mountains it was still winter, but the road was cleared to Oriana. When Slava went to the cottage, it was very cold inside. She quickly heated the accommodation, burning wood in the fireplace. She put the electric heater on, boiling water for tea. She had just covered the table with a cloth when someone knocked on the door. Slava thought that the teacher must have seen the light in the windows of the cottage while on his way to the church. She opened the door and saw the teacher. He looked alarmed. He entered the room and saw Nadia, who was preparing sandwiches for dinner. The teacher looked around curiously as if someone else might be there…

Slava said, "Teacher, let me introduce my friend who came to visit me. Her name is Nadia, and she is a journalist from the Voice of America. Please come and join us for dinner. We have just arrived, after a full day of traveling…"

The teacher nodded as a sign of greeting, and then he looked at Slava, said, "You need to leave the apartment for some time and do it as soon as possible—even tomorrow. In New York, as you know, Kovalenko's family lives, they are members of our church. They have been in Oriana on Christmas. You remember them, they are very nice people. I phoned them and they agreed to take you for a while. It is not safe for you to stay here. While you were in Washington, unknown people arrived here and asked about you. Yesterday here at this cottage a car with New York license plates was here all day. I approached them and wondered who they were and what they were doing here. The two men didn't introduce themselves and said they were waiting for you. I suspect that these strangers want to do something wrong to you. I told them no one is living here. They got into the car and drove away."

Slava silently thought about what the teacher had said to her. She was concerned about it. She hadn't expected that anything could threaten her in America. And suddenly, some unknown people without any warning or agreement had come to her home and asked about her. Obviously, her address was known to the press agencies in America; it was in the address book of the Foreign Press Center in Washington, DC, and New York, and on the Internet site too.

Nadia looked at Slava, her eyes widened… Slava was surprised, and said, "I do not know these people. I did not expect anyone to visit me, and I didn't make arrangements for a meeting… Nadia came to visit me, and yesterday we agreed that I will temporarily live at her house near Washington, DC. She came with me to help me carry my stuff. We are leaving this cottage tomorrow morning. I decided to ask for political asylum."

The teacher carefully looked at Slava. His wise eyes radiated kindness and compassion for her. His balanced and quiet voice said, "To my mind it is the only right choice in your situation. If you decide to do this, I must tell you that you are a brave woman. I am pleased to hear that you have a friend who wants to help you. Yes, in Washington you will have more chances to get political asylum. I will write to the US government a letter of recommendation, which you will send with the applications to US Immigration Services. If you need assistance, please contact me, and I will support you as much as I can. And ideally, you have every reason to get the status of political asylum. But we must be persistent, to follow your goal. We live in such a time that on the earth, everyone must fight for a place under the sun. Remember: everyone has an equal right to get that place, but not everyone gets it... The winner is the only one who deserves this victory. And you deserve it. Do you know why? Because the truth is on your side. You suffered for the truth; you have written many articles and a book in which there is a clear image of truth. You were not afraid at times of distorted notions and artificial ideas during the limitations of human thought, despotic systems of holding people in bondage. You give people a ray of hope that all is not hopeless in this life that you can understand the world differently, being free. And from those early rays, the people woke up and wanted to know what had been hidden from them for centuries. They want to know themselves, the world, and the eternal laws of Mother Nature. And they seek to live in harmony with the spiritual and material world as their great ancestors lived. This is the meaning of life on Earth. And you realized it with your noble soul, with all your heart. You deserve for me to consider you my spiritual daughter. I want to pass on my knowledge and wisdom that I learned traveling the world in search of truth. You wrote a book about me. You've read everything that I have written. But that's not all. I have not said something. The time will come, and you will tell humanity what I did not have time to say."

The teacher's words impressed Slava. Her brown eyes were full of tears. Her friend Nadia watched respectfully, with confidence that the teacher was the new messiah. Her eyes focused and showed full agreement with what he said.

On the table the tea was lukewarm. The room, overcome by some amazing life-supported power, suddenly became warm and comfortable, which was not usual for winter. The teacher went to the door, saying that it was late and he must go to the church. He would come the next morning to say good-bye.

Slava came to the teacher, bowed, and said excitedly, "Dear teacher, thank you for everything. It seems there are no words to express what is in my heart. I am very touched by your words. I just want to say that I always admire you. Yes, you are the great teacher for all humankind, not just for Ukrainian people, who do not hear or understand you. But the time will come when you will be heard. And I will do my best to spread your words to all people who seek the truth in this world."

"Slava, you are tired. You need to have a good rest, because a long journey is in front of you. See you tomorrow. Good night." The teacher bowed and left, closing the door.

Slava hastily gathered her belongings. Although she had had them for several years, it was not much, and she filled only two suitcases. Books and some of the clothing she decided to leave. She felt that one day she would be back, because the teacher was there. He was now eighty years old, living alone, and could not see well. He needed help. When she lived in Oriana, the teacher had taught her to drive his car, and she always went to the shop for food in the nearest town, Middletown. The teacher did not like to go to the shops. So when Slava could successfully cope with it, he trusted his car to her. She had often taken the car on business trips to New York for various press conferences, meetings, and presentations. She recalled at that moment the busy days when she had finished work on a book and written newspaper articles at the same time. She did not even have time to cook meals. She sat at night in the library in the church, working with archives, trying to finish in time to complete and send the manuscript to the publisher. The teacher treated her to coffee repeatedly. She just had coffee and ate cheese sandwiches while working uninterrupted on the manuscript. To her it was the most delicious of all meals, better than the food in top restaurants.

Slava recalled: one day while working on the manuscript, she smelled the pleasant aroma of fried potatoes. She unexpectedly heard the voice of the teacher, who called her into the kitchen to eat fried potatoes, which he had prepared. She had never had such delicious potatoes. The teacher ate very little. On the plate there was a little potato and a piece of black bread with butter. Slava had the same portion. This seemed like simple food, not delicacies—each of them had a small portion, but it was quite satisfying. Above all, you do not feel hunger and can work productively after such a meal. She learned how to eat healthfully—to eat little but to eat healthful food such as brown bread with bran, porridge oats, buckwheat, wheat, millet porridge with pumpkin, corn *lemishka*, vegetarian soup, vegetable soup with beans, various salads, baked apples, fresh and dried fruits, nuts, and more. All these foods had been traditional for Ukrainians since ancient times.

Slava remembered her work for the church as among the brightest moments in her life: she loved working at the church and helping the teacher. She was pleased that she had done a lot during this time. She had helped the teacher publish his book. She edited, prepared it for printing, read the computer typesetting, wrote a monograph about him as his biographer, and published many articles and interviews with him. Everything she did, she did from the bottom of her heart. She realized the importance of her work. She felt a respect for the teacher as someone who had a particular mission in life. It seemed to her that only the teacher could understand her, could give correct advice, as though she were his daughter. He treated her habits or weaknesses, but he also always pointed out that the perfect man should not repeat his mistakes; he should learn from his mistakes, making them only once. He was supersensitive—most advanced, in her understanding. He had the energy of a superman: his light energy was strong and balanced, and his view was enough to understand the world in the best sense and to feel the essence of the human in the natural purpose—spiritual growth, and self-improvement.

He felt the world in all its beauty and ugliness, which are surprisingly united and opposed like magnetic poles. He saw the world as an X-ray. At the same time he was a man of the earth who was deeply concerned about the pain of all mankind and knew how to save the world from global catastrophe. He wrote about this in his books, effectively and simply describing the complex phenomena that occur on land, in space, in distant worlds. He felt that disharmony had mastered this world, though he remained himself and tried to tell people the truth that was hidden by dark forces to manipulate the human mind and keep the world in chaos. The teacher said that until people learn to be men, they will have no future on this earth. But the biggest victims in the world among nations of fraud, deception, manipulation of human consciousness, and the destruction of memory and spiritual substance, the teacher believed, became the descendants of the Aryans, Trypilians, Scythians, Ants, and people of the Kingdom of Rus – Rusychi. Living on the richest land, they were descendants of ancient tribes, and were responsible for the cruelest destruction in the history of mankind. To take away the human memory, cripple the soul permanently, disrupt the integrity of the spiritual and the physical substance of the people, his relationship with the experience of the past—what could be worse on this earth? This was the most terrible crime against humanity.

Slava was thinking. She had learned all that from the teacher. Previously, she, like many others, had not known the truth about her country's past. Giving the true facts of the past in her articles, she referred to the authoritative sources of world-famous historians, archaeologists and linguists, and the teacher had pointed to these sources. He found them in the famous libraries of Europe, Asia, and America as proof of the statements he gave in his holy book *Maha Vira*. Obviously, the teacher himself did not need the evidence; he felt them on a subconscious level. He had a gift of providence, higher knowledge, which was transferred to him by his ancestors. He himself mentioned it in his poetic work, "A Guest from the Temple of Ancestors."

> I came from the Temple of Ancestors, from Trypillia.
> Fifty centuries I was wandering…
> The thought loved by me, I draw
> From the source of the Spirit of my Ancestors…
> The Ancestor's Spirit said to me to open

The Gateway of Historical Truth,
The nation, born in jail, to wake…
I came to visit the people.
I'll visit and go back again.
The sensitive souls and thoughts, and bones
On the altar of the Motherland I lay…
Do not rush! I came from the Temple
Of native Ancestors of saint Rus.
Greet me, brothers. Today
I am yours, and you are my tears…
I came because this is the will of Heaven,
Will of the truth, the earth, and the centuries.
I don't need either fame or gold.
The strange rash lust to me…
The light power embodied in me
Of Ukrainian Steppe heaven.
The Mother Rus' taught me intellect
That I will rise by wisdom of freedom!

Yes, he had devoted his life to collecting authoritative sources worldwide to confirm his knowledge of ancient history of Ukraine only to convince people of the rightness of his judgments and predictions.

In her publication "Who Are You, Ukraine?", published in Ukrainian-American newspaper "Viche", Slava wrote, "We know from historical sources that our far ancestors - Trypilians, Aryans, Scythians, Ants - who lived on the vast territory from the

Carpathians to the Don and from Polissia (the present territory of Belarus) to the Black Sea, were the first in the world to domesticate a horse; and they were the first to grow grain and make bread from grain: the wheat grains are considered a gift from God Dazhboh. They invented the plow and the wheel, created chariots and wagons, learned to ride horses, mastered weaving, pottery, and bronze ovens, and introduced the world's first alphabet and the written Vedas. The Vedas meant Book of Knowledge or Wisdom Books; the Sanskrit word "vid", used not only for knowledge but for understanding, is the root of Vedas. The Aryan Vedas consisted of nine books, and were dictated by our ancestors. The keepers of ancient sacred texts - volkhvs (supreme priests), in due time were to convey conserved knowledge, having carried them through millennia and preserved as much of it as possible. The Vedas contain in-depth knowledge about nature, and reflect the history of mankind on our planet Earth in the past few hundred thousand years – at least not less than 600,000 years. They also contain predictions of future events to 40,176 years in advance. These unique manuscripts were written in Sanskrit. The Indian Vedas constitute the four most sacred books of Hinduism – the Rig Veda, Yajur Veda, Sama Veda, Atharva Veda. According to academics the Aryan tribe, a group of people with fair skin, invaded India from the territory of ancient Aryan Empire, from the North of the Black Sea (present-day Ukraine), probably 5,000 years ago... The Aryans brought with them Vedas to India. The name Aryan means "royal" or "noble", "people from Heaven". Because these people believed themselves to be better than the indigenous peoples, the caste system was devised to prevent them from becoming "contaminated" by the darker-skinned natives. The Aryans established themselves as the highest caste. "They in particular brought with them the horse, the taming of which perhaps their chief immediate contribution to civilization; they became pioneers in cavalry and light-wheeled chariotry. They were more warlike than the sedentary agricultural peoples in the lands they invaded, and all had an aristocratic society, in which chieftains were prominent", wrote Herbert J. Muller in his book "Freedom in the Ancient World", 1961, New York.

Slava argued, "The Trypilians really didn't imitate anybody: they were the original creators of the first manifestations of civilization in Europe. The white people's culture and civilization began not on the banks of the Nile, and not on the banks of the Tigris or Euphrates (Mesopotamia) but on the banks of the Dnieper River. The tribes that launched Egyptian culture and civilization at that time lived in Oriyana (prehistoric Ukraine).

"The Aryans were the cradle of the Indo-European race. The Western world recognized the scientifically proven fact that from the ancient territory of Ukraine in different times came the tribes of Celts, Latins, Germans, Pelasgians, Phrygians, Balts, and Slavs to the West, and Sumer (Sumerians), Aryans, Persians, and Hittites to the East. This was proved by historians from Europe, America, and Asia… For example, the leading historians and archaeologists Jacquetta Hawkes and Leonard Woolley, in their 1963 book *Prehistory and the Beginnings of Civilization, History of Mankind,* volume 1, p.387-389, placed "the map of peoples' wandering in the Bronze Age." The map indicated the names of the people who came out of the territory of Oriyana (Arrata, Aryan Empire, prehistoric Ukraine), passing through the Caucasus to the south: Sumerians or Sumer (location: ancient Mesopotamia, modern Iraq and Kurdistan), Mitanni (northern Mesopotamia), Kassites (ancient city-state Babylon, present-day Iraq), Persians (present-day Iran), and Hittites (ancient kingdom of Anatolia, today part of Syria and Lebanon, Hittites [Hatti] means knights). They were children of Oriyana, their language, according to the scientists, was the original Sanskrit - the language of Aryans; the most ancient and perfect among the languages of the world. Hittites, Sumer, Mitanni, Kassites, Persians are Aryan tribes of Indo-European stock.

"Another well-known historian, Geoffrey Bibby, in his book *Four Thousand Years Ago,* also included "the map of Ancient Peoples," which shows the ancient territory of Ukraine. From its territory went the Mitanni, Kassites, Sumer, Hittites, Anglo-Saxons, Teutons, and Latins.

"The Ukrainian scholar O. Pritsak attributed the creation of the Tripolye (Trypilian) civilization to the alien tribes from the East, and almost all historians in Ukraine do the same. They stubbornly ignore modern archaeological discoveries; they twist the facts to suit the current official version of history. One may ask why. And to the Ukrainians who do not know the answers to important questions, one may ask, "Who you are, Ukrainians?"

"The Encyclopedia of Ancient Civilizations" in 1980 stated: "The question as to where the Indo-Aryans originally came from is bound up with that of the original home of the Indo-European languages. This subject has been under discussion since the western discovery of Sanskrit and the establishment of the Indo-European family of languages, and it will no doubt long continue to be discussed. An earlier theory of a central Asian home has now generally been abandoned in favor of a location in the continent of Europe." (p. 182).

In her publication Slava wrote, "To orient oneself in the antiquity and originality of the Trypilian culture and civilization, it is worth mentioning the following dates: ancient Greeks and the Jewish people appeared on the horizon of history about 3,100 years ago; before this date nobody mentions them. The ancient Romans (Latins) were younger than the Trypilians—their history began about 2,700 years ago. So taking into account the archaeology, the history of European culture and civilization began on the banks of tributaries of the Dnieper, north of the Black Sea. And our ancestors were not "savages," as they were called by falsifiers of history, for which the history of Ukraine begins from the baptism of Kievan Rus (988 A.D.); they say our ancestors were "barbarians" and that "Greeks brought the culture of Byzantium to them." They could not bring them something they did not have. One of the Aryan tribes—the Pelasgians—came from the north of the Black Sea to the territory of present Greece probably 5,000 years ago, determined to live not as outcast settlers but as masters in a land of their own. The ancient historian Herodotus wrote that Pelasgians lived in Greece before the invasion of Greek tribes. And as world science proves, our ancestors at one time were the most advanced people on the planet Earth."

Slava stated, "I found an article by Walter S. Sullivan, published January 19, 1973, in the *New York Times*. The well-known American journalist and science writer wrote that "horses were domesticated in the steppes of Ukraine more than 4,350 years before Christ." This scientific discovery was made by scholars Rainer Berger and Rainer Porch from the University of California in Los Angeles. In the above-mentioned newspaper there was a map of Eurasia that showed the settlements of Ukraine: Usatovo, Dereivka, and Yevminka. The bones of horses, harnesses, and the wheels of carts were found in excavations of the territory of the Ukrainian villages by the archaeological expedition.

"The leading Canadian expert in Ancient history, Senior Researcher Andrew Gregorovich, of the University of Toronto, provided a significant analysis of the origin of Ukraine and the Ukrainian people in his publications. He stated that the earliest horse known to be ridden by a man was 6,350 years ago near the Dnieper River in the central Ukraine at Dereivka. In his study "The Origin of Ukraine" Andrew Gregorovich made conclusion that "the overwhelming majority of archeologists, linguists, historians and other scholars place the origin of Ukrainians, Slavs and Indo-Europeans on the territory of Ukraine… As a result the Ukrainian nation is autochthonous, because it originated on the territory of Ukraine… Some scholars suggest that Ukraine's history actually starts with the highly developed Trypilian Culture in 3,000 to 5,000 B.C. which left traces in Ukrainian culture. We can also start Ukrainian history with the early archeological evidence of agriculture and the use of geometry in Ukraine which goes back over 40,000 years…"

Slava wrote, "There are lots of these sources, and oddly enough, the scientific discoveries and findings about prehistoric Ukraine were first made by foreign scientists, and they wrote authoritatively about them in their publications.

"Not long ago, in Ukraine was found one of the oldest monuments of the spiritual life of ancient Ukrainians: the Rock Mound (Ukrainian: Kamyana Mohyla, literely: Stone Tomb) in the Zaporizhzhya region, whose unique inscriptions and drawings (petroglyphs) are considered the oldest of all that have been found in the archaeological world. So, we can conclude that the oldest writing emerged in Ukraine, that the history begins not in Sumer (an ancient civilization and historical region in southern Mesopotamia, modern Iraq), which is considered to be the official history, but in the territory of modern Ukraine. Yet Ukrainian historians ignore this discovery, because it requires the review of still existing ancient history, and European scientists ignore this discovery also, perhaps because they don't know of Ukrainian sources and have only limited access to them.

"The world's leading Sumerologist Samuel Kramer, a Ukrainian born American historian, in the 1963 book 'The Sumerians: Their History, Culture, and Character' asserted: "The history begins at Sumer..." But he was wrong because he did not know about Kamyana Mohyla; the archeological discoveries were made later. According to Encyclopedia Britannica, "Sumer was first settled between 4,500 B.C. and 4,000 B.C. by a non-Semitic people who did not speak the Sumerian language." Wikipedia stated: "During the third millennium B.C., a close cultural symbiosis developed between the Sumerians (who spoke a Language Isolate) and the Semitic Akkadian people, which included widespread bilingualism. The influence of Sumerian on Akkadian is evident in all areas... Sumer was conquered by the Semitic-speaking kings of the Akkadian Empire around 2270 B.C., but Sumerian continued as a sacred language. Native Sumerian rule re-emerged for about a century in the Third Dynasty of Ur..." (The word 'Ur' means a habitable and fertile territory; and 'Sumer' means native land. According to the Vedas and Sumerian legends, Urs came from the planet Urai; Urs had mighty abilities far beyond the imagination of the majority of ordinary people, and they became tutors and guides to the rest of the people. Urs trained people and helped them to master primary technologies, and gave them the knowledge necessary for them at that moment as well as knowledge that would be called for only in millennia. Sumerian people were Aryans who came from the plains north of the Black Sea.)"

Slava stated, "Thousands of years before Sumer was founded, and millennia before the first stones of the pyramids of Egypt were hewn, the Trypilians (Tripolye peoples) were building their cities in the land of ancient Ukraine, north of the Black Sea (this is the birth place of the Sumerian, Vedic and Egyptian, and European civilizations). They built circular cities, sacred pyramids, astronomical observatories and had hieroglyphic writing, the world's first and oldest writing. These ancient peaceful farmers and artisans had a culture that was strikingly similar to the culture of Atlantis. Recently the sacred pyramid sites were found in Ukraine which archeologists have dated back an estimated 20,000 years. Twenty thousand years ago the magnificent Atlantis was still a thriving empire, long before the Atlantis disappeared beneath the Sea of Azov and the Black Sea, in 9,600 B.C. According to Ukrainian archeologist Yuri Shilov, "The Aryan's earliest Myths make an intriguing account of archeological findings in the steppes north of the Sea of Azov and the Black Sea; archeologists found observatories, calendars, temples and enormous figured fashioned as humanlike and astral deities. The myths of Ukraine turned out to be very close to those recorded in the Indo-Aryan Rig-Vedas. This fact corroborated the linguistic conception that Aryans and their beliefs had originally came from the lower Dnieper area in Ukraine, north of the Black Sea…"

Slava wrote: "In well researched illustrated book "Atlantis Motherland", published in Hawaii (USA), authors Leon Flying Eagle and Mary Whispering Wind present the evidence that the history of Atlantis is true, and the true location of Atlantis had finally been solved. Numerous theorists have attempted to locate Atlantis literally all over the globe. "Atlantis Motherland" emphasizes the common heritage of all Human beings and the origin of our ancestors, and the probability of extraterrestrial interbreeding with primal earth tribes. The idea is that humanity originated in the area of Eastern Europe north of the Black Sea, in Ukraine. Retelling of Plato's histories of Atlantis is combined with modern scientific investigations, discoveries and intuition; (Plato [428 - 347 B.C.] was a philosopher in Classical Greece, student of Socrates, one of the most dazzling writes in Western literary tradition, author of the Atlantis Dialogues, and founder of the Academy in Athens.)

"The authors of "Atlantis Motherland" asserted that Atlantis, contrary to what is commonly accepted, was located in Eastern Europe north of the Black Sea, a large island covering a big dry area, now known as the shallow Azov Sea, located in Ukraine. The book emphasizes that one of the most mysterious treasures of Atlantis, the predecessors of Aryans, is a sacred archeological site known as Kamyana Mohyla (Rock Mound). The stones of Kamyana Mohyla rest in an awkward heap along the western shore of the Sea of Azov, near city of Melitopol, and are referred as the stone library, because the stones are covered with petroglyphs, etched by our far ancestors, recording thousands of years of human history. There are many ancient tales of wonder and magic surrounding these ancient stones. Kamyana Mohyla is considered one of the oldest temples in the world, which was gifted to us from our ancestors. Many of the petroglyphs are more than 9,000 years old, and some of the petroglyphs are more than 20,000 years old. Prehistoric carvings are clearly visible. These stones depict the story of a great ancient flood, and may be the first recorded history of the Great Atlantis Flood… People from Hyperborea had supposedly settled Atlantis.

"Only one third of the sacred stones of this ancient temple Kamyana Mohyla by the sea have been viewed in our modern times. Projects are being formulated to gently lift the giant stones, one by one, then carefully document the petroglyphs and tenderly replace into them in position, just as they have rested by the seashore for many millennia. For now the stones rest under the guardianship of Stone Grandmother (Kamyana Baba), female stone idol. They stand in front of this ancient stones of Rock Mound, watching over the history of beginnings of civilization, which was recorded in this pile of rocks. The treasures of Atlantis will be revealed at the proper time...

"The legend of Atlantis has mystified myriads of explorers, for thousand of years. Now it is a physical reality. The mystery of Atlantis is finally solved. The Island of Atlantis lies beneath the Sea of Azov, north of the Black Sea. The Metropolis of Atlantis was on top of a hill in the center of a great plain. This hill is now above the sea. It is the Hill of Mithridat in the center of the Crimean City of Kerch in Ukraine. Currently accessible beneath this hill are ancient quarries, catacombs and rooms as mentioned in ancient Atlantis history. Ruins of ancient tower foundations and remnants of massive stone walls are clearly visible underwater in Kerch Strait. The Island of Atlantis was actually artificially created the primal Atlantis. They utilized the natural features of the land, and excavated an incredible ditch, around a vast fertile plain, thus creating the Island of Atlantis. The empire of Atlantis was destroyed by the forces of nature. A massive earthquake caused the entire island to sink. Then a massive flood inundated the vast farmlands of Atlantis, which are now buried under 11,600 years of accumulated alluvial slit, beneath the Sea of Azov. The lost ancient advanced civilization of Atlantis is the common Motherland of all Humans. These discoveries will instigate a tremendous stimulus to the cultural life and spirituality of Ukrainian people, as well as to the economy of this area, and unite the one world family for peaceful co-existence.

"Another unique event became the latest research in archaeology, and stunned the world with its sensation. The scientific discovery was made by Ukrainian archaeologist Alexander Yanevych based on findings from excavations in the Buran-Kaya caves, near Yalta on the Crimean coast of the Black Sea. In the scientific journal *PLOS One* from June 17, 2011, we can read that the age of the first Europeans is bout 32,000 years. The unique findings of the archaeologist Yanevych were confirmed by scientists from around the world. Specifically, they conducted a series of radioisotope datings of Yanevych's archaeological findings. First they were conducted in Oxford, but they also conducted research in laboratories in Holland and Paris. The results of all of them showed that the age of the findings was more than 30,000 years. The study of Yanevych's Crimean findings gives reason to believe that the first European—a "wise human being"—lived in the territory of modern Ukraine, and from there spread across the continent. Yanevych's research proved that he found the remains of people in the Buran-Kaya caves who in anatomy were similar to modern human beings. It was the oldest find of its kind in Europe.

"Ukrainian historic science keeps silent about these important facts—significant archaeological discoveries in present-day Ukraine—with the aim of hiding the truthful knowledge from people about their roots, their past, and their oldest culture. And the awful stuff that historians do in Ukraine—they deform and rewrite the history in their own way that has nothing to do with truth. This is a crime: they believe that before Christianity there was no history. And where did the ancient belief disappear to? It still remains in the sacred Vedas… There is a reference in the ancient chronicle about the bloody baptism in Kievan Rus: *volkhvy* (ancient priests), Rusychi (people of Kievan Rus), who did not want to betray the native belief, were annihilated by Prince Volodymyr and his hired army. The number of sacrifices of those who did not accept the Christian religion in Kievan Rus amounted to three million. It was just one of the many tragic pages of the history that withdrew from our memory...

"Aryans tribes - Etruscans and Pelasgians - inhabited Italy and Greece, founded Troy, and created a demographic concept that does not allow overpopulation of the Dnieper land and the Chornomorsk (Black Sea) steppes, inhabited by many families of the Aryan tribes. Volkhvy (supreme priests) from time to time arranged a drawing, as a result of which the young community of settlers went to new lands. So some ancient families settled in India, Iran, Iraq, Pakistan, Palestine, Egypt, Italy, Greece and other Western European countries, and on the island of Crete.

"Referring to the statements of the spiritual teacher Dr. Lev Sylenko, as a superior scholar of ancient history in free world, today we can say that ancient Ukraine (Oriana, Arrata) is the most probable homeland of the Indo-Europeans, and that the old Ukrainian language is the basis, the primary source, of Indo-European languages. The ancient way of the Aryans, who carried the farming culture, can be traced in the following areas: Oriana (present-day Ukraine, Belarus and Russia), India, Mesopotamia, and Western Europe. As the first civilized people on Earth, the ancient Aryan people came to the fertile valleys of the Tigris and Euphrates 5,300 years ago and turned Mesopotamia into a blooming paradise. The village Rusa-Salem (Jerusalem) was build by the old

Orian (Aryan) tribes. It is known that the creators of Buddhism and Zoroastrianism—Buddha and Zarathustra—originally were Orians (Arians). Dr. Sylenko wrote about it in his book *Maha Vira*, in which we read the following lines: "I stated it in the name of truth and conscience of historical science, not racial, national or religious feelings, pride or exclusiveness." While researching this work Dr. Sylenko journeyed to Greece, Crete, Turkey, Iraq, Iran and India. He also travelled to Mexico and Central America with the purpose of doing scientific research on the history of Toltecs, Aztecs and Mayans. He worked on his book for over twenty years. As a historian, linguist and indologist, he had spent several years compiling a Sanskrit-Ukrainian-English dictionary, a work which would be of great value to linguisticians and scholars of ancient history and culture. The newspaper "Time of India" (Bombay, February 9, 1975) published a well-wishing editorial article about him. The Director of the Research Institute of Sanskrit at Sampurnanand Sanskrit University in Varanasi, Dr. Vagish Shastri, after receiving Dr. Sylenko's dictionary, wrote, "This is an interesting specimen of intercultural language link." In his research Dr. Sylenko came to conclusion that the study of Sanskrit led to the comparative study of languages. It was found that Sanskrit, Persian, Greek, and Latin, and also the Celtic, Germanic, and Slavic languages come from a primitive unwritten language called Orian (Aryan). From Ireland to India, and all over Europe and America, Aryan languages are spoken. (Dr. Sylenko's merits are noted in the American Biographical Institute bicentennial edition (1975-1976) Community Leaders and Noteworthy Americans, and in The International Who's Who of

Intellectuals, 1981, volume 2-3, International Biographical Center in Cambridge. He was nominated for the Nobel Prize in literature as Author of a unique book, Maha Vira.)

"The historian and archeologist Jacquetta Hawkes stated, "The obscure question of the expansion of Indo-European languages and of the various groups of peoples who spoke them must be discussed before closing this attempt at a unified view of the prehistory and early history of the Old World... It is now widely agreed that peoples speaking related languages, much concerned with cattle raising and using horse-drawn wagons and chariots to give them mobility in peace and war, radiated out from home lands lying in steppe country north of the Black Sea between the Carpathians and the Caucasus." ("Atlas of Ancient Archeology", 1974 p. 12)"

Slava wrote in her publication, "The known historians Grahame Clark (University of Cambridge) and Stuart Piggott (University of Edinburgh), in their book *Prehistoric Societies* (1965), reported that "5,500 years ago, Central and Middle East (India, Iran, Pakistan, Mesopotamia [present-day Iraq], Palestine and its neighboring lands) were conquered by tribes that are native, which lived in the rich plains between the Carpathians and the Caucasus." And further: "When we come back to the early grain-growing settlements, we find the presence of greater ties with Tripolye (Trypillia, ancient Ukraine) than from the Ancient East (Mesopotamia)." Historians Grahame Clark and Stuart Piggott stated that Aryan tribes started the history of agrarian culture before the Sumerians (Sumer) came to Mesopotamia; they wrote: "Pottery with incised decoration, figurines of women and domestic animals, and copper objects have been found. Dating is almost guesswork, and it seems difficult to place the culture much before 3,000 B.C., if as early, although Carbon 14 dates for allegedly successive phases would push it back into the fourth millennium B.C., unless we could allow an overlap between this and the main manifestation of what is called the Tripolye culture, from a site near Kiev."

Slava stated, "Professor Roman Ghirshman of the Sorbonne in Paris, a Ukrainian-born French archeologist and head of many archaeological expeditions, in the 1965 book *Iran*, says that the space to the north of the Black Sea is the motherland of Indo-European people. The historian John Bowle in the 1977 book *Man Through the Ages*, wrote that Aryans came from the territory of Ukraine.

"A prominent investigator of the ancient world, historian Ramesh Chandra Majumdar, in his book *The History and Culture of the Indian People* (in the part "Vedas era") wrote that Ukraine more than any other country (countries of Europe and Asia) may claim to be the earth of Aryans. The German home theory is popularized very much in many European schools for racial justification. We know that based on German home theory Adolf Hitler proclaimed that the Germans belong to the higher race because, 'Germany is the Motherland of Indo-European race'. It should also be mentioned that there is some early pseudo-scientific literature, especially German, which is distorted and anti-Slavic. But, in fact, a German scholar, Otto Schrader, in his 1890 book "Prehistoric Antiquities of the Aryan Peoples", which is the first classic study of this issue, placed the Indo-European or Proto-Indo-European origins in South Russia from the Carpathian Mountains east. (Historians sometimes call the territory of Ukraine as 'South Russia', 'North of the Black Sea', 'Tripolye' [Ukrainian word Tripolye or Trypillia means Three Fields], basins of the Dnieper, Dniester, Bug and Pripet Rivers).

"American scholar, Professor Marija Gimbutas, in her work "The Slavs" described the Slavic origins in Ukraine in this fragment: "Initially an insignificant, repeatedly subjugated Indo-European group living north of the Carpathian mountains and the middle Dnieper river area, the Slavic farmers through their persistence managed to survive and ultimately succeeded in occupying a vast territory in Central and Eastern Europe and the Balkan Peninsula." (p.14). Professor Marija Gimbutas also stated that in 1887 and 1908 the Polish botanist Jozef Rostafinski fixed the original Slavic land in Ukraine through analysis of the names of trees and placed it in Ukrainian Polissia, the basin of the Pripet River. This Beech (Ukrainian: Buk) tree theory is considered untenable by Professor Henrik Birnbaum of the University of California. In his 1973 paper at the International Congress of Slavists in Warsaw (Poland), Prof. Birnbaum stated: "The first area identifiable as the Proto-Slavic homeland would therefore have to be located somewhere in… the present-day Ukraine, just north and probably north-west of the Pontic steppe and the black soil belt, i.e., the hinterland of the northwestern shores of the Black Sea. Such a conception is… also in general agreement with the view, based primarily on archeological evidence but taking into due account also linguistic and historic data, expressed by Professor Marija Gimbutas" (Journal of Indo-European Studies, Winter 1973, p. 411).

"Robert G. Latham, a linguist who investigated Sanskrit, in the book *The Ethnology of Europe* stated that Sanskrit language is of European origin, it spread in Asia up to India... Aryan came from ancient Ukraine far before the birth of Christ.

"The "New Encyclopedia Britannica Micropaedia" (1998) places the origin of the Indo-European languages exactly in Ukraine: "The Indo-European languages are the descendants of a single unrecorded language that is believed to have been spoken more than 5,000 years ago in the steppe regions north of the Black Sea..." (vol. 6 p. 296). Most of the languages in Europe such as English, French, German, Italian, Spanish, Greek, Polish, Ukrainian, Belarusian, Croatian, Serbian, Bulgarian, Czech, Slovak, Macedonian, and Slovene are Indo-European. According to researcher Andrew Gregorovich, Indo-European as a term to designate the major family of languages in the world was coined by Thomas Young in England's Quarterly Review in 1813. At the time it was thought that all these languages originated with Sanskrit in India. But it should be mentioned that the term Indo-European is misleading since it seems to indicate that these languages originated in India and spread to Europe. In fact the scholars have determined that the Indo-European (or Aryan) languages originated in Europe, on Ukrainian territory, about 5,000 B.C., and expanded west across all of Europe and south-east to India. Some scholars have placed the origin of the Indo-European and Slavic people exactly on Ukraine territory but have not mentioned the name Ukraine, they used 'South Russia', because in the past Ukraine was the part of Russian Empire. For instance, historian Herbert J. Muller in his book "Freedom in the Ancient World" (1961) wrote:

"Scholars now prefer southern Russia as the most probable homeland of Indo-Europeans." Historians and archaeologists Jacquetta Hawkes and Leonard Woolley in their book "Prehistory and the beginnings of Civilization, History of Mankind" (1963) stated, "Tribes of Indo-European stock, originating probably in South Russia, left their homes for some reason that we do not know and, passing through the Caucasus, poured eastwards and westwards, an armed host accompanied by their wives and children, in search of a new places wherein to live; and they were determined to live not as outcast settlers in an alien land but as masters in a land of their own… One wave of the 'Aryan Invasion' in time broke through the mountain barrier of northern Baluchistan into India." (p. 387-389)

Slava stated in her publication, "The eminent British archaeologist Stuart Piggott in his book "Ancient Europe" (1965) wrote: "If we look at the archaeological evidence from what we can broadly call the south Russian region [present-day Ukraine] in the middle third millennium B.C. we do in fact find communities of copper using agriculturalists who would perfectly well fit the philological necessities so far as they go. Settlement sites, such as that of Mikhailovka in the lower Dnieper area [Ukraine], provide evidence of copper-using agriculturalists, reaping and grinding a presumptively cereal crop, domesticating cattle, sheep, goats, and pigs, and either hunting or taming horses, and living in villages of timber-built thatched houses… There seems to me to be a good case for suggesting an equation between the linguistic evidence for an assumed Indo-European homeland between the Carpathians [Ukraine] and the Caucasus, and the archaeological evidence for people whose material culture and chronological position would fit the philological requirements in that area... And when we turn to west and north of this region we find, in the last few centuries of the third millennium, widespread evidence usually interpreted as implying the spread of new people whose affiliations are broadly with the south Russian [today Ukraine] area we have just discussed... Over much of east and central and central Europe, on the north European plain, in Scandinavia and Holland, we have, cutting across the traditions of the Danubian long-house villages and their successors, the appearance of what appear to be new peoples whose pot forms, with a plentiful use of ornament made by impressing cords into the surface, their shaft-hole stone battle-axes buried with their warriors as weapons of prestige..., all seem to show relations with the regions north of the Black Sea [Ukraine]." (p. 54-55, p. 81-84).

Slava wrote: "Vere Gordon Childe, known as V.Gordon Childe, was an Australian archaeologist and philologist who specialized in the study of European prehistory. Working most of his life as an academic in the United Kingdom for the University of Edinburgh, he wrote many influential books such as "The Dawn of European Civilization" and "The Aryans: A Study of Indo-European Origins". In 1926 V. Gordon Childe represented the first really solid synthesis of research on the Indo-European origin since Otto Schrader, German scholar. "Having surveyed all other regions of Europe we turn to the South Russian steppes [present-day Ukraine]," said Childe. Extensive archeological research in Ukraine the past half century actually strengthens the choice of Ukraine by academic Childe who thought the horse was a key factor in Indo-European expansion. Childe also thought the perforated battle-axe design with a hole in it identified the Aryans and many examples have been found in Ukraine. Even the ancient Egyptians didn't think of this logical axe design. The kurgan burial mounds and the "ochre-grave folk", said Childe, were Indo-European and there were huge numbers of these in Ukraine.

"In his book "The Down of European Civilization" (1957) V. Gordon Childe wrote: "On the loss-clad flanks of the Carpathians, in the valleys of the upper Oltu and Seret, and on the parkland plateau extending north-eastward across the Prut River, the Dniester, and the Southern Bug to the Dnieper, there developed, on a Starcevo foundation enriched by Danubian elements, a remarkable farming culture named after Tripolye, a site near Kiev. Though its authors were throughout farmers and lived in large villages of substantial houses, they seem, like their kinsmen farther west, to have practiced a sort of shifting cultivation. Hence the village sites are very numerous – twenty-six have been identified in 110 sq. miles just south of Kiev…" (p. 136).

Slava wrote: "Russian scholars such as Aleksey Shakhmatov have also placed the origin Indo-European and Slavic homeland on the territory of Ukraine. Josef Safarik, a Slovak scholar, in 1837 located the original Slavic homeland in Ukraine. The famous Czech archeologist, historian and Slavist, Lubor Niederle, in 1902 have placed the origin of the Slavic people in the middle and upper Dnieper River territory in Ukraine.

"The greatest thinker of modern India, Sarvepalli Radhakrishnan, in the book *Indian Philosophy,* wrote that Aryans brought with them certain concepts and beliefs, which they continued to develop in India.

"Dzavaharlal Nehru, former prime minister of India, in the book *Discovery of India* says that the Aryan group comes from the wide spaces of the Danube, Dnieper, and Don.

"American authority on Ancient History, the author of "A History of the Ancient World", Chester G. Starr wrote: "The discovery that some elements of the group had moved in early times all the way across the Near East to India was one of the greatest achievements of the modern study of comparative philology. As British officials and traders in India became acquainted in the eighteenth century with Sanskrit, the early sacred tongue of that vast peninsula, they found that it had clear ties with the language of Western Europe. Throughout the nineteenth century philologists explored the fascinating ramifications of this fact and fitted into it other linguistic findings so as to create an impressive panorama of prehistoric movements of Indo-European peoples across the northern and central stretches of Eurasia." (1974, p. 81).

Slava stated, "Today scientists in the free world have proved that the characteristic features of Trypillia (Tripolye, Tripoli) culture are most clearly seen in the heirs of Aryan tribes – Ukrainians, and their language probably is the oldest language in Europe. The Ukrainian people do not know about this. They are manipulated by distorted, misleading information and alien people's beliefs about the world. Their true knowledge was hidden deeply for thousands of years. And it is not surprising that among the Ukrainians, the teacher was born and came to Earth to awaken the nations and give them true knowledge that, like unsolved mysteries of time and space, came to us from long ago. He combined ancient knowledge with the modern requirements of time, based on those realities in which we live today. He predicted a big step forward for mankind: evolution as the beginning of a new era, the era of light. It returns, but moving forward as a circle, as the eternal law of recurrence, as the golden age of its time. Many thousands years ago, our great ancestors experienced the Vedic knowledge of the world, the most perfect knowledge of human civilization on the planet Earth.

"The teacher passed his knowledge not only to Ukrainians, but also to the whole of humanity. He thought in terms of a higher level of spiritual development of mankind. He predicted that in the future, mankind will move from the materialistic idea about the world. The teacher said that today more than ever we need a revaluation of spiritual values. He suggests that when people awake, they will realize God's original purpose for them encoded in their genes and passed on from the spiritual ancestors of a Vedic knowledge and the ancestors' past experience. The gradual transition that is happening now at the higher level of human development on Earth, the current competing religions and distorted idea of the world that leads to chaos and confrontation. In the future people will have one faith in the creator of the universe, and it was predicted by the teacher: he gave a new system of world ideas, which has its origins in Vedic knowledge, by reforming the multi-gods' faith of Rusychies, our ancestors. Probably the views he had on peace and faith will be for future generations. There were many gods that were multiple manifestation of one god in the ancient faith of the Rus, and they had their own image and gender (that is, images). The teacher can see a future understanding of God-Creator as eternal energy. Dazhboh in his understanding is light, love, truth, and eternity."

Articles with similar content were published in many newspapers in Ukraine and Ukrainian Diaspora in the United States, Australia, Canada and Great Britain. In the West people are free to express their opinions in the press or in books, and no one is prosecuted for their articles. But in Ukraine there is secret censorship, which is hidden in the governmental structures that define what the Ukrainians are allowed to know and what they are not allowed to know. That is how the social consciousness is completely controlled. The teacher could write his books and freely express his ideas while in Canada or in America or traveling in the free world. Slava wrote her articles and a book in America, and they were published in Ukraine. Of course, nobody expected that a former teacher of Taras Shevchenko Kiev State University, with PhD degree in Slavic philology, would write such "revelations" about America and about the ancient history of Ukraine. They didn't expect that she would recollect that once in Ukraine there were glorious ancestors, who were the creators of perhaps the first manifestation of culture and civilization in the world, and they were not "barbarians" or "savages"; on the contrary, they spread their advanced culture—Trypilian agriculture and domestication of animals, weaving, and pottery—all over the world, and from them the language and the first spiritual centers of the white man were introduced in Europe. Among the Ukrainian people appeared such a person who was simply Teacher, who wanted to return to the Ukrainians that which was hidden from them for centuries, the true knowledge about their past.

Slava was sure she was doing everything correctly as a journalist and was not acting contrary to professional ethics: to write the truth and only the truth. She really wanted to disperse the myth among the Ukrainians about "rotten" America that had spread during the time of the Soviet Union and continued to evoke in the heads of Ukrainians an echo of the past. Obviously, the negative influence of Soviet propaganda had worked, and by inertia continued to exist as an echo of the Cold War. But the decisive reason that Ukrainians even today are not allowed to know the truth about their history, their ancestors, and about a better life in the West is their dependency on their northern neighbor: the centuries-long oppression, particularly the Communist-Soviet oppression, was still felt. Slava repeatedly asked herself: why there was still resistance in people's minds since Ukraine had become independent. After a long search and observations, and communication with different people with whom she met as a journalist, she came to the conclusion that Americans have very positive attitudes toward Ukrainians, especially since the Orange Revolution. Among ordinary Americans she never noticed even a hint of any hostility to the new emerging country with a young democracy. Obviously, they did not accept the breach of human rights and corruption in Ukraine, and they reacted to the events, taking the relevant resolutions of the Senate, voicing the position of the US government through the Department of State, or giving an assessment of the relevant events in the White House.

Slave instinct of self-defense against pro-Western propaganda works in Ukraine as a manifestation of chronic disease, which unfortunately does not lend itself to treatment at present. Therefore, the pro-government structure in Ukraine in favor of the "big brother" role of its northern neighbor Russia continues to believe in inertia that Americans are their enemies. In Ukraine there very rarely appears a pro-Western leader, and they attempt to remove that person from the political Olympus of the country very quickly by different ways, acceptable and unacceptable. The hero of Ukraine's Orange Revolution Viktor Yushchenko, the former President of Ukraine, was poisoned. As an informal leader of the Ukrainian opposition coalition, he was one of two main candidates in the October-November 2004 Ukrainian presidential election. Viktor Yushchenko won the presidency through a repeat runoff election between him and Viktor Yanukovich, the government-supported candidate. The Ukrainian Supreme Court called for the runoff election to be repeated because of widespread electoral fraud in favor of Yanukovich in the original vote. Viktor Yushchenko won in the revote (52% to 44%). Public protests prompted by the electoral fraud played a major role in that presidential election and led to Ukraine's Orange Revolution. Following an assassination attempt in late 2004 during his election campaign, Yushchenko was confirmed to have ingested hazardous amounts of TCDD, the most potent dioxin and a contaminant in Agent Orange. He suffered disfigurement as a result of the poisoning, but has been recovering in recent years. Russia has made no secret of its dislike for Viktor Yushchenko , who has pursued a firmly pro-Western policy aimed at membership of NATO and European Union. The former Russian President, Dmitry Medvedev, has condemned Ukraine's pro-Western course and said he looked forward to better relations under a new president of Ukraine.

Slava belonged to the youngest generation of Ukrainians who had witnessed incredible events, including the declaration of an independent Ukraine. She knew many of her contemporaries—who were journalists, academics, politicians, and economists—in whom she saw the potential creators of the new Ukraine. All of them were united by a sincere desire to rise to higher standards of living by getting rid of the inferiority complex that had become ingrained during the Soviet occupation, and they wanted to build a free Ukraine, comparable with the European benchmarks of a democratic society.

The older generation brought up on the Communist propaganda of a slave experience of survival under any conditions became an obstacle to the aspiration of these young people, who were full of desire and energy. Members of the older generation of former party leaders were promoted to almost all senior positions in the country, not giving a chance to the younger generation. They further ruled the independent Ukraine, continuing the old traditions and Soviet orders, and following the Soviet lifestyle. They had a fear of anything new; they just were not ready for the requirements of time and the new changes. The stereotype of the Soviet people worked there: they used the time for themselves, robbing the country and pocketing enormous wealth. And for this purpose they created a corrupt criminal environment in the country in order to protect their interests and gain material wealth in different ways, legal and illegal. These people had unlimited power in this country, and the level of corruption in Ukraine today is one on the first places in the world. The living standards of ordinary people became incredibly low, even lower than during the Soviet Union's time, which led to high levels of crime and moral fall of the society as a whole. More than two million young Ukrainians emigrated abroad, seeing it as the only way to get rid of this terrible reality. Slava knew many of the younger generation who remained in Ukraine, and their fate in most cases was tragic: they either died, voluntarily or forcibly, suffered from alcohol abuse, or simply adapted and became similar to others, living in impoverished distress or watching some become enriched at the expense of poor and disadvantaged people.

When a country is in such terrible condition, and you can see it all for yourself, feel it yourself, and are anxious about your family who remains there, it is natural to wish to do something about the situation, to help in some way. In her life Slava was guided by the principle of objectivity, the conscious desire to convey to readers information that was concealed, distorted, or falsely highlighted in the Ukrainian media: she wanted to show readers the current level of perception about the situation from people living on another continent who also have families and care for them, want to live in harmony and peace, and have all that is necessary for a normal life. She believed that all people around the world should not be divided on the basis of religion, politics, or race. Mankind is the only family of the only planet called Earth. She wanted to say that all people living on Earth have a joint house and one common problem: how to live in harmony in this common home.

In America you see for yourself how many nationalities, ethnic groups, and religious groups can coexist. Everyone keeps and cherishes their culture, faith, or tradition, yet they all share common human values and secular humanism. In her articles Slava showed the best aspects of American life and how we can take a positive experience to learn something, to reject something, to leave the negative stereotypes in the past that were created during Soviet times. Obviously, Americans also had their own problems, but generally they adjusted their lives and were satisfied with what they had. And oddly enough, because of Slava's professional career as a journalist, her family in Ukraine began to be harassed and intimidated. The message was that she must stop writing anything associated with America, an indication from the top editor of the newspaper that her articles would not be published…

These recollections on Slava's fate and the hopeless situation that prompted her to seek political asylum in another country did not let her sleep until morning. At dawn she fell asleep for a few hours. She was awakened by a knock at her door. She dashed out of bed, put on her coat, and opened the door. It was the teacher. He held an envelope in his hands.

"I came too early, but I promised yesterday to present my letter to the US government to grant you asylum," he said. "You can enclose it with your application when you send it. I will leave for a while for

Canada and be back in about a month. Give me your phone number so I can contact you," the teacher said.

Slava took her notebook, quickly found Nadia's home phone number, which she had recorded only the day before, and dictated it to the teacher. He put the note into his pocket, wished her a good journey, and then said, "Slava, you must be very careful…"

Slava looked down and shook her head. She saw the small suitcase by the door.

"Teacher, are you leaving today?" she asked.

"Yes, I am in a hurry to catch the coach to New York. In thirty minutes it will be in Spring Glen, and my next bus to Toronto will depart at eleven this morning" the teacher said.

"Yes, I know—at eight thirty the bus will be here. And the next one is at four o'clock," Slava said anxiously.

Nadia proposed to the teacher that they all can go to New York together by her car.

"Teacher, we will drop you at the bus terminal at 42nd Street."

The teacher agreed, and within a half hour they all left Spring Glen by Highway 209.

It was the last day of February, and the coming of spring could be felt. The bright sun was warm. The snow lying on the roadside melted quickly. The storks could be seen in the sky over the mountains through the car windows.

"You see—storks are flying in the sky. The spring and warm summer are arriving earlier," said the teacher. "These birds bring the warmth. We have considered the stork from far ages as a sacred bird of fate and happiness. There is a sign that the person who sees these birds coming first will be lucky all year-round. This sign is very good for you, Slava. This means that these noble birds positively affect your destiny. I am sure your asylum case will be resolved successfully. Go confidently your own way, and your intentions will certainly come true. Your fate is in your hands. You and only you are its creator. You define it by the energy of your opinions."

These words of the teacher touched Slava, who was immensely happy in this unforgettable moment. She understood what it meant to have a great faith... Then the whole world will turn to you: give your energy of good to the people around you and it will be repaid to you a hundred times. This is the best feeling when you receive this award from others, giving them your own.

New York was seen from afar. They quickly reached the Lincoln Tunnel, one of the longest tunnels in America, which connects Manhattan to the mainland. Just as you leave the tunnel, you find yourself in the heart of this gigantic city with its huge skyscrapers. Nadia parked the car at 42nd Street in front of the Port Authority Bus Terminal. Slava and the teacher went to the bus station. They bought the ticket to Toronto and immediately rushed to the bus, which was leaving in fifteen minutes. Slava went ahead so the driver could wait for the teacher. When the teacher caught the bus, the driver closed the door. The bus moved slowly. Slava saw the teacher wave his hand in farewell. She really wanted to go along with the teacher, to accompany him. He was an elderly man and had to lean on a stick. But she could not go at this moment.

Slava returned to the car, where Nadia was waiting for her. Slava carried a box of pizza. Nadya smiled, "It's good timing... I managed to buy a little. There is a shop not far from here—can you see it? There are Italian shoes. I bought two pairs of good shoes for spring. Can you imagine? I paid half price. In Washington, I would not find such cheap shoes. Maybe you want to buy something for yourself?" asked Nadia.

"No, that's all right. I have everything I need. I bought pizza baked in brick oven in Bertucci's Italian Restaurant at the bus station. Help yourself," said Slava.

In about five hours' time they were already in the Nadia's house in Silver Spring. Nadia was cordially met by her husband, who had returned from a business trip. She introduced Slava to him.

"Slava needs some help, and she will stay with us for a while," she said to her husband.

He nodded and invited her to dinner, cooked by him.

During dinner, they chatted, and Slava talked about herself. George, Nadia's husband, understanding Slava's situation, said that he could help with her asylum case; he had many friends who could suggest something useful.

"So we will begin tomorrow," Nadia said.

"Slava, are you ready? We will go together to the Voice of America, so take the application forms with you; you can fill them out there. How is your English?" Nadya asked.

"I can speak good English. I taught it in school, at the university, in a graduate school. So I can fill out the application, but it would be good for you to check it when I do."

"Well, in my room where I work, there is a free desk with a computer. You can do your own business there."

The very next day, Slava went with Nadia to the Voice of America offices. Nadia's room was very small, but there were two desks with computers. From the window you could see a beautiful landscape with a view to the White House, which was very close. It was eight o'clock in the morning. Slava sat at a free desk to fill out the application form. First, she carefully read the questions on all fifteen pages. Then she began to answer questions on a separate sheet of paper. She focused on each answer and used the Ukrainian-English dictionaries for translation. Slava did not notice as the time approached for lunch. Nadia offered to go with her to the cafeteria on the ground floor.

After lunch Nadia invited Slava to the main office of the Voice of America editors. It was a big, spacious room, with several tables with computers and technical equipment. The editor in chief, whose office was next to this room, was there, as well as three journalists. Nadia presented Slava as the first accredited Ukrainian journalist in the United States. They looked at her curiously, came up and greeted her, and everyone shook hands. These well-known journalists had worked in the editorial office for years. Slava was pleased to meet them. The editor in chief put a chair in the middle of the room and offered it to Slava.

"At first, we will introduce ourselves, and you tell us about yourself. We are so glad you are visiting us…," said the chief, and then he smiled. "My name is George, and I am an editor in chief of the Ukrainian Service of VOA, and these are our famous journalists, senior editor Yuri, and filmmaker Slavko."

"I have read your articles in Ukrainian newspapers," said Yuri. "It is interesting how you write. Your thoughts are innovative—I would say fresh... I just returned from Ukraine. I worked there as an accredited correspondent from the Voice of America for almost a year. I could not stay there longer; I received threats by phone from anonymous people."

"You received threats...?" Slava's eyes widened.

"Yes, and oddly enough, in Russian language... Can you imagine? In Kiev, the Ukrainian capital, I was threatened in a tongue I almost do not understand. I was born and brought up in Chicago in a Ukrainian family. But I understood what they told me. They demanded that I leave Kiev immediately and return to America, and to not do anything with American propaganda... I didn't do propaganda. The only stuff I did was preparing reports from Kiev for the Voice of America network as an independent journalist. I met Ukrainian politicians, journalists, and ordinary people. I did not feel any hostility toward me as an American. Instead, they were hospitable and kind people. All the people I knew talked to me in Ukrainian. You can see, they threatened me in Russian. I understand that the part of the population in Ukraine that considers itself Russian and speaks the language are a small minority; they set their rules in a country that for them is foreign. In the government they are much more than ethnic Ukrainians, I noticed...," said Yuri.

"Do you know, I agree with you," Slava said. "Indeed, in the government there are many people who speak the language of their northern neighbor, Russian. But still there are Ukrainian people who have their national dignity and who speak their native language in any circumstances. But these people in their native land are called nationalists, or Bandera. So, Ukrainians can't freely speak their parents' language in their native land. There is something wrong about it."

"You are right," George said. "You know that Ukrainians for centuries were in captivity. The northern neighbor always hammered into the heads of the Ukrainians that they are the worst people, and incapable of running their own country… It is its own kind of incurable pathological disease. Do you know, my father said, it is difficult to be a true Ukrainian…? Do you remember the poem by Lesya Ukrainka, the most revered woman writer and cultural figure of Ukraine? 'I don't have a fate, or freedom…,' she wrote. Ukrainians suffered some unhappy fate. They were constantly destroyed and persecuted, the native language was forbidden—and how many Ukrainians died during Stalin's purges and famines? I think that the real genocide of Ukrainian people is going on, but worst of all, the Ukrainians don't notice it. They gradually assimilate with the northern neighbor, the slave habits become the norm, and no one protests… This seems to lead to the disappearance of Ukrainian ethnic groups, if they do not realize what is going on," the chief said anxiously.

Yuri nodded. "We, Ukrainians in Diaspora, know what is happening in Ukraine… We translated and published many books in America about what is actually happening in Ukraine, and also spoke openly about it on our radio networks Liberty and Voice of America. We also published the works of Ukrainian writers that were forbidden by the Soviet regime. At the expense of Ukrainian

Diaspora the newspapers in Ukrainian is published in America. The older generation of immigrants has tried to keep Ukraine even here, across the ocean; they have remained as Ukrainians in exile. Moreover, they have built their own small Ukraine. Do you know how many Ukrainian organizations are here?"

"Yes, I am acquainted with the life of the Ukrainian Diaspora in America. I wrote an article about it and it was published in Ukraine," Slava said.

"I see you have a medallion with a trident *[tryzub]* in the sun. Is that your faith?" asked Slavko.

"Yes, it is my faith," said Slava.

"Oh, you have to know the teacher, who founded the Native Faith Church," said Slavko.

"I wrote a book about him; it was published in Ukraine. I also recorded an interview with him in the Ukrainian newspapers," said Slava.

The editor in chief said he remembered the teacher from Germany, where they had been together in a camp in the American zone.

"At that time we knew him as a great humanist, a defender of human rights, a passionate speaker, and a talented writer. He published several anti-Soviet books. He was a brave man, a unique personality… You are saying that you wrote a book about him… Well… Did you know that thanks to this man the Ukrainians from Germany could emigrate to America after World War II?" asked George.

"Oh yes! I wrote about this event in my book. The teacher told me that after the war, Ukrainians who were in displaced-persons camps in Germany were not allowed to go to America. There was the applicable law—the author was Senator Pat McCarran—under which people who worked in the Soviet Union territory were regarded as having strengthened the USSR, and so they were unwelcome in America and deprived of their right of entry. This meant that the Ukrainian victims of fascism were facing the threat of deportation to the USSR, where there waited the NKVD torture chambers and Stalin's concentration camps. Many Ukrainians were taken to the Soviet zone by force, and they have become innocent victims of this inhuman law. It seemed that salvation would not come; many people fell out of the trains in which they were taken or finished their life in suicide so they would not get into the hands of the NKVD. And one brave Ukrainian defended all who were insulted. He wrote an Open Letter to the American People, which was translated into English and published in American newspapers. This letter was distributed by influential Ukrainians among senators and congressmen, and it was sent to all the leaders of the European countries. The author of this letter was Lev Sylenko, whom people later called simply: Teacher," Slava nodded.

"This is actually the case," George said. "It's only one tragic page in the history of Ukrainian immigration, but this letter made a noble cause in favor of Ukrainians, and thanks to Sylenko, my family could come to America. And not only mine—thousands of similar people."

"I wondered how that story had ended. I didn't know anything about it," said Nadia.

"It ended up that Lev Sylenko announced a seven-day hunger strike in protest of this inhuman law, and he wrote about it at the end of his 'open letter,'" Slava said. "On the sixth day of the hunger strike he was taken to the hospital, so his life was saved. Then a miracle happened: McCarran's law was withdrawn. Lots of Ukrainians started to emigrate to the United States. This was the second wave of Ukrainian immigration, which is called post-war political emigration."

"Here is an interesting story for our television program *Window on America*," said George. "I have planned for a long time to make a video of the teacher…"

The editor in chief looked at Slava for a moment and then said, "Now tell us about you. What brought you to our editorial office? What can we do for you? I have read about you in the newspaper *Svoboda (Liberty)* and found out that you are the only accredited journalist from Ukraine."

"I was invited to your editor's office by my colleague…" Slava smiled and looked at Nadia. Their glances met; they understood each other without words.

"Imagine, we met by chance at a press conference in the Press House last week," Nadia said. "I invited Slava to us, because she needs our help. The fact is, Slava is submitting an application to US Immigration Services for political asylum. Yesterday she moved from New York, and now she is staying with me."

"Slava, you were threatened like I was when I worked in Kiev… I am familiar with this situation. They did not like your articles. I also read about it," Yuri said sympathetically.

"They not only did not like my articles, they intimidated my family. My father was met on the street by an unknown person who threatened him and then pushed him so hard that he barely stayed on his feet. The editor of the Ukrainian daily newspaper *Molod Ukrainy* was ordered not to print my articles anymore, and I was sent anonymous threatening letters. All sorts of nonsense were written about me in Russian newspapers, saying that America paid me a lot of money to spread American propaganda," Slava said.

"Yuri, you will be the first witness to confirm that you have also received threats in Ukraine…," offered Nadia.

Yuri smiled briefly and nodded without taking his eyes of Slava.

"In this situation we need not only one witness," the editor in chief said. "There must be numerous facts proving that Ukraine persecuted journalists for their professional activities. We have to see what we have in our archives. We should also go to radio network Liberty. They probably have materials about the missing journalists, about the retribution, intimidation, and threats. And we must turn to Freedom House. They make a report on human rights violations in different countries… And one more very important fact to remember: I have read the report *Reporters Without Borders*, in which the president of Ukraine entered the top ten enemies of the press as a result of last year's report. Of course, for Ukraine, which only began its democratic path, it is very bad, but for you, it is a strong argument for obtaining political asylum status.

"But note my advice: keep what you are doing a secret. It is necessary for the security of your family who remain in the country from which you now seek refuge, and to which you may not return. They can put pressure on your family to prevent you from doing so… And do not talk about your personal affairs over the phone. I am sure they may bug phones. When you get your status, you should bring your family to America to avoid any surprises," saying these words, George gazed at Slava. He knew that anything could happen in that country.

Slava at that moment felt excruciating pain in her heart as she further realized the risk she was taking. There, on the other side, remained the people most dear to her: her daughter, her mum and dad.... It was only now that she realized she would never be able to return. Before her she saw a clear image of her mother smiling. Her mother touched her head and began to do her hair as she did when Slava was a little girl...

"Slava, are you all right? I think you are pale. Shall I bring water?" asked Nadia.

"No, thank you, I am okay. I would rather send applications."

"Do not worry. We will help you… If we need to, we will turn to the Senate with a request to support you," said Yuri.

"The status of political asylum in the United States is not easy to obtain," George said. "Only about a hundred people each year receive this status. The US government takes care of refugees and provides full support; all opportunities open to them to become a full citizen of this country. You have a chance to make the immigration deal in your favor. As the Americans say, welcome to America!" Then the editor added, "You can come to our editorial office and help with the literary editing of our programs; you will be our freelance journalist."

"Thank you, George. Your support means a lot to me. Yes, I accept your proposal," said Slava.

For her it was a pleasant surprise. She saw that there were people around her who understood her and were ready to help. Above all, she never felt alone.

A week later Slava sent all the application forms to the US Immigration and Naturalization Services office, which was in Nebraska.

Two months passed very quickly. During this time, Slava had the opportunity to explore American life closely. She liked American pragmatism, a rhythm that was as clear as an electronic clock, the life of Americans and their looseness, friendliness, open style in communication, simplicity, and honesty in relationships between people. She settled into this adjusted pace of life in which there was no room for anxiety, worry, or alarm. She went to the editorial office almost every day. She liked to be there and to feel that there were people who would not leave her with her trouble, who were always ready to help. It was her first spring in Washington, DC. In March the magnolias were blooming; cherry trees bloomed in April, and many spring flowers were planted in parks, in flower beds on the street, and near public institutions.

Slava had a lot of free time to walk down the wide streets of Washington and along the embankment of the Potomac River at Kennedy Center and Watergate. She visited the Lincoln Memorial, which is in a large park. She thought she was in another world that lured her with its charms, spices, and the smell of spring flowers. Her nature sought that beauty, and she wanted to call out loudly, "People, what a beautiful life! Keep the beauty of your soul. Do not destroy yourself by the indifference to this world..." What could be sweeter than a breath of freedom? She felt herself a free person. No one dictated or commanded what she should do; no one persecuted her or intimidated her. She decided for herself how to live...

The one thing that did not give her peace was the thought of her family in Kiev. Slava telephoned her relatives several times a week. She felt that her parents were worried about her. Her family did not know at that time that she was seeking political asylum in the United States. On the phone she did not go into the details of her private life; she told them almost nothing. She wanted only to hear of the voices of people dear to her; she was worried that something would happen to them. She worried most about her daughter. Every day she thought about her and believed that one day they would be together again...

In early May she received a letter from Nebraska from US Immigration Services. It informed her that she was going to have an interview in the local Immigration Services office in two weeks. She had been looking forward to this piece of mail. And at long last, the day had come. It was May 21. Slava was going with Nadia and Yuri by car to Annapolis, where the immigration office was. The interview was scheduled for nine o'clock in the morning.

It rained heavily all the way; the rain did not stop until they were in Annapolis. Nadia joked, "This is Ukraine crying for you, Slava... Do not worry, you will see, everything will be fine. You have got the evidence, the proof is serious, the editor's office gathered the documentary evidence, and, most important, you have a strong witness... Look, Yuri, do not let us down. We're relying on you. You are with us as a lifesaver in case of drowning."

"Nadia, you'd better stop somewhere to buy coffee," Yuri said.

"We are nearly there; we have little time left. It's fifteen minutes to nine, and we still need to find a parking space…"

They entered the premises of US Immigration Services, and at exactly nine o'clock, Slava was called for an interview. The staff member said they would call her witness later on if necessary. Slava was invited to a small room. The woman, who was of Chinese origin, was following her. She introduced herself and said she was authorized to conduct the interview. She asked Slava to stand, raise her right hand, and repeat the oath after her to tell the truth and only the truth. Then the immigration officer asked Slava to put on the table all the documents she had with her. She had the folder with the application form that Slava had sent two months earlier. She checked her passport and collated it with the application. Then she asked whether Slava had a document confirming her accreditation in the United States. Slava gave her the certificate from the Foreign Press Center and showed her the center's reference book, which contained a list of all accredited journalists from around the world in the United States, including the information about her. The immigration officer asked if Slava had brought along the original newspaper that had published the articles that were mentioned in her application. Slava took out several folders and papers and passed them to her. Since the articles were in Ukrainian, the officer said that at least two or three of the articles should be translated into English. Then she asked Slava the same questions that were on the application. Slava felt that this woman was favorable to her and treated her kindly. It was easy for Slava to answer all the questions in English, because she had prepared herself for two months before the interview.

When Slava finished answering all the questions, the officer said she didn't make any decisions herself and that the process of obtaining this status needed to go through the immigration court. Only the judge could decide, based on the evidence and testimony of witnesses, whether to approve this request or not. This was only the first stage of a long process. The officer explained that this was the same process for all those who sought political asylum, and that in approximately two to three months, a letter from US Immigration and Naturalization Services would be sent that would tell what she should do next. When the interview had ended and Slava rose to leave the room, the employee shook her hand in farewell and wished her good luck in the conclusion of the case.

Slava's friends had been sitting in the hall, waiting for her. When they saw her, they immediately rushed toward her, asking, "How are you? What happened in there? Will they call me as a witness?" Slava reassured them and explained everything the Immigration Services worker had told her.

The teacher called in the evening. He asked how the interview was and also said he had received a letter for her from Ukraine that he wanted to send to her new address. Slava told him that it was just the beginning and that now she needed to prepare herself for the immigration court, because, as was explained to her, only the judge was authorized to decide whether to satisfy her request or reject it.

The letter from US Immigration Services she was expecting came about two months later. It said that Slava was invited to immigration court in early November. It was necessary to find a lawyer immediately. There was a list of charitable organizations that helped in immigration cases for free by providing legal services and consultations. Slava phoned almost every number on the list. Most of these organizations were of religious orientation: Catholics, Baptists, Muslims... Not surprisingly, they politely refused to take up her political asylum case. The first thing they asked was which religion she belonged to. Slava told her friends at the editor's office of Voice of America (VOA) that she couldn't find a lawyer through those organizations that had been recommended to her. Then Yuri telephoned a friend who was a solicitor of Ukrainian origin. The lawyer suggested that journalists should contact the organization Freedom House, because they probably knew how to deal with these things. He himself didn't practice immigration law, so he couldn't touch this case.

Slava remembered that she was a member of the International Women's Media Foundation, and that she had been at a press conference with Suleima, a well-known journalist from Iran, who also sought political asylum in the United States because of her persecution at home. She even found her phone number in her notebook, because they had kept in touch. Slava telephoned Suleima, who advised her to contact the legal clinic at Georgetown University.

The next day she went with Nadia and Yuri during lunch to Georgetown University. They were cordially greeted by Professor Barbara Brown, the dean of the Law School. She carefully listened to them and then asked Nadia and Yuri to leave her alone with Slava.

Barbara asked, "Do you have a fear of returning to Ukraine? What do you fear most?"

Slava replied that she most feared becoming a victim in a country where there was no justice, where they persecuted and killed journalists, politicians, and dissidents just because they told the truth about the crimes of totalitarian corruption of authority, the crimes of Communists, who destroyed the Ukrainian masses in their native land by famine and repression, simply because they loved their country and defended their right to freely live in this country and speak their language, know their true history, because there is no nation without a past and there is no future without a past...

Professor Brown asked Slava to show her the articles she had written. Slava put the folder with the papers and her book, which she had brought with her in a small suitcase, on the table. Barbara smiled and said she did not know the Ukrainian language but could read Russian, which she had learned in college, so at least she could read Slava's name and the title of the articles.

"Well, you have proof that you actually wrote articles for newspapers and published a book. Now it is important to prove that you were truly threatened and therefore are afraid to return to your country of origin, where you were born," the professor said.

"This is the newspaper, published in Kiev, where my honor and dignity were humiliated," Slava said. "Without any grounds I was accused of being paid big money by Americans so I could write these articles, as they say, to spread American propaganda… These are letters from my father in which he mentions that our family was intimidated and suffered harassment because of my professional career. My father was threatened, so I stopped writing my articles. There is a letter my father wrote telling me that an officer from Security Service came to his place of work and demanded that I return to Ukraine. A chief editor of *Youth of Ukraine* wrote me a letter, which I received the other day. He mentioned in it that he had received the instructions from above to forbid my article to be printed… and they demand to cancel my accreditation in America and say he must to do that in order to stay as chief editor of this newspaper."

"Yes, this is really good evidence that you cannot return. Do you have a visa?" asked Barbara.

"I have an A1 business visa, which allows me to stay in America as long as I have accreditation as a journalist. This certificate is from the Foreign Press Center and indicates that my accreditation expires in three months' time. And to renew the accreditation, I need an official letter from the editor, certified by the US embassy in Kiev."

"Your case requires immediate consideration. We have to submit your case to the court within three months, so you won't be deported. Today there is a meeting of our faculty. I will offer your case, and after the meeting I will phone you with the result. I hope that your case will be of interest to my colleagues and we will meet soon. Good luck to you!" the professor said. She smiled kindly and shook Slava's hand.

After seven in the evening Slava received the phone call she had been waiting for. Professor Brown said they had decided to take the case and made an appointment for her to meet with professors and students at nine o'clock the following morning.

Slava came to the university a half hour early. She really liked the architecture of this prestigious educational institution, which was famous for its graduates and was considered one of the ten best universities in America. She wanted to look closely at the Gothic buildings, which from afar resembled a majestic medieval castle in a modern design. The territory of the university was not possible to walk around in half an hour, so Slava took a short walk around the central administrative building. At exactly nine o'clock she was already in the lobby of the Law School of Georgetown University. She phoned Barbara and said she was already in the lobby but needed a pass to go through. A few minutes later, two students came up. They took Slava to a spacious room next to the library. There were professors and students waiting for her. Once Slava came in, everybody paid attention to her and watched her with curiosity. Barbara came up to her, smiling kindly, gave her hand, and introduced Slava to all presents.

Slava was a bit uncomfortable as all gazed at her, as though learning who she was. Professor Brown noticed it and said confidently, "As I already told you, we should immediately start to work on the case to protect this brave journalist from Ukraine, who is not afraid to speak out against her country in defense of her human rights to fairly defend her principles in her professional activities. She has turned to us for assistance. We don't have much time to prepare her case for the court hearing. She has very good grounds for winning the case. She convinced me of this. Now we must convince the judge that the return of this journalist to Ukraine is dangerous. The case is serious: her father was threatened, and she was asked to stop her professional activity. They asked the editor to not publish her articles and to deprive her of accreditation in this country, to publish libelous material on her, and to find a cause for accusations. They threatened her, demanding that she return to Ukraine. Our professional duty, dear colleagues, is to protect this young, talented woman who is a victim of injustice and antihuman, cruel rules that still exist in this post-Communist, most corrupted country, where the young democracy is only beginning to develop."

Slava was touched that this American woman, whom she had just met the day before, had so frankly and openly started to defend her. She felt a particularly friendly atmosphere, and an attentive and sympathetic attitude toward her. She thought she was in the right place among these good, noble people who behaved so naturally with her. She felt comfortable, surrounded by people close to her, as if they had known each other a long time.

"This is the group of your protection," Barbara said to Slava, indicating with her hand all the people in a circle around the table. "Professor Goldenberg is chairing this group. He is the dean of the Department of International Law, and he is a big man," she said jokingly. Then Barbara introduced Professor Highland. He stood up, bowed, and gave his hand to Slava, because he was sitting beside her. Indeed, he was a tall man. He tried to look sympathetic: he smiled and also joked that Irish people are tall like Ukrainians (Slava was a tall woman, and he was of Irish ancestry). All the people laughed.

"And these are your true advocates and advisers, Abigail and Sandra," Barbara said. "They have already completed Law School and now they are undergoing the legal practice. This is the first case they will prepare for the court. They will be your advocates. As you can see, this strong and experienced team will work for you with one goal: to win the trial. We had a meeting of the faculty and included your case in the program as educational practice for our university. So before your official court hearing, we will have a rehearsal with the faculty of law for educational purposes.

"Well, now we have to prepare the plan of our training program to the court. We are ready to start working with you tomorrow. As you know, we hope to have full understanding, cooperation, and assistance between you and our advocates. You need to submit all information that you have, listen to their advice, and follow their recommendations. You have to understand that this is only in your best interest... Oh, sorry..." Barbara looked at the clock, and continued: "I am leaving you because I have a lecture now, and my students are waiting for me. You can explore this more closely and discuss an action plan for the next weeks... And do not forget that we have limited time. Good luck! See you!"

Slava was aware of the schedule of work for several weeks in advance. The provisional meetings were set up for every day except on weekends. She was warned that all her interviews would be recorded on video for later use as a training program for university students. She also had the opportunity to speak in her native language, Ukrainian. Yuri agreed to translate. He offered his assistance on a volunteer basis. In addition to his main journalist job at the Voice of America, he worked as a translator for the State Department, interpreting for the president of the United States during his visits to Ukraine as well as for official delegations. Yuri had the highest qualification of the interpreters, but he always had spare time to help Slava. When Yuri was on a business trip, Nadia helped. For Slava they were the kind of real friends only a few people are lucky enough to find. They were next to her from day to day all those three months, until the court was held.

Almost every day, except weekends, Slava spent three to four hours at the university with her advocates. She gave her testimonies, which were recorded on video. In the meantime, Slava's parents were invited to the American embassy, where they video-recorded an interview. Yuri went on a business trip to Kiev and helped invite her parents to the embassy. He translated their testimony into English. Also in Kiev, Yuri helped to find those journalists who were threatened and even fired from their jobs for their professional activities. Some of them served time in jail only because they wrote the truth about the crimes of criminal authority, and they openly talked about it in interviews for radio Liberty.

Slava spent a lot of time in the Library of Congress, where the files of Ukrainian newspapers were kept. There she found articles by journalists who were no longer alive and whom she knew personally. In the Library of Congress she met with Dr. Yaroslav Yasinski, the head of the Department of Eastern European Studies. He was of Ukrainian descent, a representative of post-war emigration, and remembered the teacher from Germany: he gratefully remembered when the teacher went on a hunger strike in defense of Ukrainians like him who were not allowed in America because it was the law, and after Ukrainian protests and the known "Letter to the American People," the law was withdrawn... He said that thanks to the teacher, he and thousands like him could come to America as political emigrants.

Dr. Yasinski helped Slava search articles about the persecution of Ukrainian writers, journalists, and politicians in the Ukrainian and foreign press. Slava later learned that he wrote as an expert. At the court's request he reviewed her articles and book, assessed her journalistic activities, and gave his opinion that at the current situation and with the current government, it was dangerous for Slava to return to Ukraine. In government circles in Washington DC, he was known as an expert on Eastern European affairs, and the official annual report of the US government on the situation of human rights and freedom of the media in Ukraine was issued based on his knowledge.

Three busy months passed very quickly. The group of advocates at the university was very active: all of them were in a hurry to collect evidence from Slava, her parents, witnesses among journalists, and victims of threats and persecution in Ukraine; various official and independent reports on the state of freedom of the media and human rights in Ukraine; and documentary evidence of the facts about journalists who was killed in Ukraine; and to make it to court. Almost all of these materials had to be translated from Ukrainian into English, and they had only a very short time in which to do it. Yuri and Nadia had to work even at night, because during the day they were busy at their jobs. They translated all the documents, statements, and Slava's articles into English. At the beginning of October, the file, which was almost a thousand pages, along with documents, videos, newspaper materials in their original language and translated into English, and photos had been prepared and submitted to the court. At the request of the judge it was necessary for Slava to undergo an examination by a psychiatrist, who was appointed by US Immigration Services. Slava was surprised that she was sent to a psychiatrist, but she was told by her advocates Abigail and Sandra that this was mandatory for anyone in a pretrial process.

The examination lasted nearly four hours. The psychiatrist put forward quite strange questions, it seemed to Slava. For example, he asked about her sense of fear, whether she had experienced fear when she was a child, and what caused fear for her, and whether she experienced depression, because in psychiatric practice, fear is the main symptom of depression. Were some people suffering from depression in her country? Why was she afraid to return to Ukraine? Did she fear for her family? Why did she decide to engage in journalistic activities? Did she expect that something similar could happen to her in her country? Did she personally know journalists who were no longer alive? What prompted her to come to America to work as a journalist? Was she going to move her family to America because of the threats they had received while she worked as a journalist in America?...

Then the psychiatrist asked Slava to tell him about herself since she could remember. She remembered her happy childhood and her good, intelligent parents. In that system you could rarely meet such people. In Soviet times people usually adapted to the circumstances to survive. Her parents had ordinary positions; there were many people like them. Her father was a teacher at the college; her mother was a pediatric doctor. But they had created a wonderful world around them of good, human perfection. People loved and respected them for their high integrity. There was understanding and respect between father and mother; we could say that their relationship was full of harmony. Slava wanted to see the world as perfect as it was in her family. But to her disappointment, this world was not as great.

Slava told the psychiatrist that she could remember herself from the age of three. She remembered the first manifestation of violence against her heart, when she was three years old and went to kindergarten. The kindergarten teacher forced children to eat their full portion of food during dinner, but if they did not obey, they were force-fed until the plate was empty. It happened to Slava once: she would not eat some porridge, which she disliked, and the teacher had force-fed her. Then she experienced the most violence in her childhood that she could remember. The same day she ran away from the kindergarten, and the teacher did not even notice. Little Slava remembered the way home and surprised her mother when she appeared on the doorstep of the house…

The psychiatrist smiled and said that she had already been a refugee in her childhood, that it was her first experience.

Slava told the psychiatrist that the atmosphere of fear is created in a society where there is violence against people, where there is humiliation of human honor and dignity, where a man is forbidden to be free, where there is infringement upon human rights. Such a society is dominated by fraud, betrayal, cruelty, violence, and bribery. Fear is born when one loses one's will or is threatened. Fear arises around uncertainty and the danger of losing one's life, which is given to a human by God. When a whole country lives in fear, its human community does not have a future. It is doomed to extinction, because this way of life doesn't have common sense and is incommensurable with the laws of the Universe, according to the Vedas.

Slava said, "I was born to be free in this world, and this privilege we received from God, the Creator. Everyone is called to defend the natural instinct for survival, and no one has the right to encroach on the most sacred right. For the person it's important to be free, to improve the human nature, to live within the laws of the Universe: no one has the right to take a person's life. It is the essence and manifestation of God on the planet Earth and came to fulfill its purpose."

Slava remembered the words of the teacher: "Man is a creator of his own destiny and no one has authority over a person." By her thoughts and actions, she created her future. She believed: "There is One God, the Creator. There exist many religions, because there are many different concepts of God." She said, "My faith is my pathway of life. My Faith is the nature of my soul. My faith is the bliss of my mind. Without my faith I cannot live, without me my faith cannot exist. My faith is my past, present and future. There are no non-believers. There is a faith with God and a faith without God. My faith is a faith with God, the Creator. Atheism is a faith without God. Faith is inspiration. The more noble the faith, the more noble is life. The more noble life, the more noble is the understanding of freedom, beauty and love. Everyone believes that his faith is truthful. If so, then all existing faiths in God in the world are truthful. No one has the right to convert or avert from his faith, whether it be by means of fire or sword. He who constitutes faith by force or by intimidation is a miscreant. A noble faith does not persecute anyone for differences in religious life and different concept of God. The level of knowledge about God depends on the level of spiritual and mental development of man. God is absolute; knowledge of absolute knows absolute only. Different concept of God should not provoke hostility among people. The differences in the concepts of God enrich the spiritual life of Mankind. Religions which have millions of believers and religions which have thousands of believers should be equally respected. There is only humanity and the grace of God, where the believers of one faith have tolerant attitudes to the believers of the other faiths. In Ukraine we have so far different reality…"

Slava told the psychiatrist that she was afraid to return to her homeland, because she recollected when some journalists whom she knew personally were killed. She remembered her student years when she attended a practical seminar in linguistics called Journalism Mastery that was taught by Professor Alla Koval, a prominent Ukrainian scientist, head of the journalism department. She was the model of a real professor of the older generation, compared with other teachers. The students were inspired by her independent disposition and intelligence, but she did not have as good a reputation among teachers as among students. In her workshop students discussed the news they heard on the radio networks Freedom and Voice of America and discussed the works of writers of the sixties, who were repressed in Soviet times. At that time it was forbidden to listen to foreign radio stations, because they were considered pro-Western and anti-Soviet propaganda, and were called "hostile voices." This workshop didn't last long; it was banned, and Professor Koval had to retire.

At the seminar Slava met with a fifth-year student. It seemed as if many years ago, she reminded herself of this young, intelligent man, who was full of energy and whose life was taken away.... He liked Slava, but although they met several times, then they separated. Slava was in her second year of study. He later became a famous journalist, one of the organizers of the youth movement in Ukraine, which actually led to a change in government. It later discredited itself, uniting with criminal groups and business clans. He began to write openly about these criminal authorities in his articles, and exposed criminal plots on television, and he paid for it with his life. He was murdered in his own apartment. And such incidents were common... He was not the only one who fought for the truth and became the victim of a criminal regime. It was that new generation of youth, which was prevented from developing, who all the way to self-realization were blocked from realistic dreams and opportunities.

Slava told the psychiatrist about another talented journalist who worked for the popular magazine *Ukraine*. He wrote articles about writers of the sixties, including the famous Ukrainian poet Vasyl Stus. It was during the period of Mikhail Gorbachev and perestroika, when there was free access to the archives of the NKVD and KGB. Slava worked on her thesis at the Institute of Literature. She wrote many articles about Ukrainian writers, victims of Stalinist repression. She brought her articles on this subject to the magazine

Ukraine and spoke to this journalist. They were good friends, and they had a sincere desire to expose the truth about the terrible crimes of the Soviet occupation to Ukrainians. They could talk for hours about the work of forgotten or forbidden Ukrainian writers from Soviet times who were missing in the exile camps in Siberia and were tortured in the dungeons of the NKVD and KGB. After many publications in the journal about the poet Stus, who was killed by the KGB, the author of these articles was found dead near his home with traces of a severe beating. The wife of the murdered journalist gave an interview to the Liberty radio network, in which she told how her husband first was threatened. Then they met her on the street and brutally warned her what to expect if her husband did not stop writing about Stus, and suddenly a few weeks after the threats he was found dead… The murder of this journalist was still undisclosed; a killer had not been found, and no one had been punished for the murder.

The psychiatrist listened to Slava's story. He thought for a moment, and then sympathetically said, "It's sad to hear such a tragic story from such a beautiful woman… Do you know, I think that the scenario of the tragic events of the journalist reminds me of the story you told me about yourself and your family before. It started with threats, intimidation of your relatives, and then… This can end up the same way as with the journalist?"

"I agree with you; this horrible scenario probably applied to many people in Ukraine," said Slava.

"I support you in your request for political asylum in the United States. This is the only right decision in your situation—you convinced me of it—and I will write about it in my report," the doctor said. He added, "I wish you success, and if you need any help from me, please contact me. I am always ready to help you. May God bless you."

His report consisted of twenty-five pages and was crucial to her case. The psychiatrist wrote everything Slava had told him. He objectively described Slava's situation and presented his findings and recommendations concerning her.

A week before the immigration court hearing, on Halloween, the university held a court hearing with the participation of students and faculty of the Law School as a study model and general rehearsal before the main hearing. It was planned as a practice for students and put into the training program of the faculty. A room at the university had been specially equipped as a courtroom, designed to all US standards. The dean acted as judge, advocates were Abigail and Sandra, and Professor Highland played a lawyer for Immigration Services. It was very helpful for Slava to have this training as preparation for her hearing. Everybody took their responsibilities very seriously as part of the educational process, and it was like a real court. The advocates were firm and active; they argued that only political asylum could save Slava from the threat to her life and that a return to Ukraine would be extremely dangerous. This role-play lasted three hours. And at the end, the dean, who acted as the judge, ruled in Slava's favor.

Then the long-awaited day of the real hearing came. It was the fourth of November in the courthouse in Arlington. The support group from the university came a half hour before the court hearing. Slava also came early, with her friends Nadia and Yuri. Exactly at ten o'clock in the morning all went to the courtroom. A few minutes before the hearing, the official representative of US Immigration Services arrived. There were two stenographers in the courtroom. All were sitting and waiting for the judge. Suddenly all stood: the judge had entered. He looked around then greeted. The hearing began. Before the judge there was a large file the size of two encyclopedic books. It was Slava's case, prepared by her advocates from Georgetown University.

First of all, the judge announced that this was a request for political asylum. The judge asked Slava to take her place on an elevated side, which was near the judge. The lawyers sat at a table in front of the judge. The court hearing lasted about two hours. First Slava briefly told the court who she was. Then the judge asked her when the persecution began, if there had been any threats, why she decided to ask for political asylum, and whether there was any threat to her life. Slava based her arguments on facts and evidence from her relatives and the editor in chief of *Molod Ukrainy*, and journalists from Ukraine who proved that her life would be threatened if she returned to Ukraine. After she gave her evidence, the defense advocates Abigail and Sandra had their turn. They spoke very clearly, as professional advocates, referring to the facts collected by Freedom House, an official report of the State Department, and many other materials.

A representative from Immigration Services asked only one question. He wondered how many journalists from Ukraine had received political asylum in the United States. The advocate Abigail explained that Slava was the first and still the only accredited journalist in America, and that there weren't any cases similar to this one. The persecution of journalists in Ukraine existed and was clearly demonstrated and documented in the documentary records, in the Ukrainian press, from evidence of journalists in Ukraine, and from relatives of dead journalists. Obviously, there was a threat to a journalist's life in Ukraine, and here was the evidence and interviews recorded in Ukraine by correspondents of Voice of America and radio Liberty. But in this case, Slava worked in America and wrote many articles about America. She was accused of spreading 'American propaganda'. They had to bear in mind that Ukraine was one of the countries of the former Soviet Union and that there were still stereotypes from the Cold War in relation to America. Her articles were banned in Ukraine, and there was the evidence from the editor of the newspaper for which Slava worked. Most important, there was a threat to her life if she returned to Ukraine and there was proof of this fact that she knew personally journalists who were no longer alive. The advocates elucidated the circumstances of the death of these journalists; none of the murders were investigated, and no murderers had been found.

The judge asked the representative of US Immigration Services if he was satisfied with the answer. He nodded and said he had no more questions.

In conclusion, the judge asked Slava where she would work if she were granted political asylum, and whether she could support herself and her family. Slava firmly answered that she would work and could maintain her family herself, and hoped she would be offered a job at Voice of America.

The judge was satisfied with the answer. Finally, the judge announced that he had decided, banging the judicial hammer on the table, "To allow the political asylum. The case is completely exhausted, and I shall declare the court closed."

When the judge was going to go away and the audience stood up, he turned to Slava and said, "Remember my name, John Kossak... Judge John Kossak. If you write a book about your life, remember the judge who made the decision to save your life. Welcome to America! May God bless you!"

Everyone in the audience began to applaud. The judge smiled with satisfaction as he went to the exit. The same moment Slava's true friends Nadia and Yuri came up to her, the advocates Abigail and Sandra excitedly began to hug Slava with joy over the successful completion of the court hearing. Slava could not resist and burst into tears of joy. Professor Highland and Dean Goldenberg, and the representative from Immigration Services, welcomed her and wished her success in settling on American land; she gladly accepted their good wishes...

On the ground floor of the modern glass building of the courthouse was a very spacious café. Nadia invited everybody to dine and ordered a large pizza. Oh, that was the most delicious pizza for Slava. It seemed to be the tastiest she had ever eaten. Her friends, Abigail and Sandra, the dean, and the professor were unspeakably happy. All of them radiated joy and satisfaction from the successful completion of the case. Yes, they had all together won the case, and the difficult daily work, sleepless nights, worries, stress, and constant tension in waiting for the hearing were behind them.

"Slava, you have to write a book about your great victory. Did you hear what the judge told you?" said Sandra, not hiding her emotions.

"Yes, I definitely heard it. I know that we won together. And I will always remember your help, professionalism, humanness, and kindness... I just do not have words to express what I feel... I am going to write a book, if not now, then later. This book will be called *Freedom*," Slava said.

"Today was perhaps the biggest event in your life," dean Goldenberg said. "You are now a free person. America has opened the door in front of you... I would ask you to maintain contact with us. We are curious to know how you arrange your life in the future. We will be happy to learn about your success, and if you need help from us, you can always contact us... Now you will go with your advocates to the immigration office on the second floor, to fill out an application for a work permit.

"Here is the original decision of the judge; this is your main document showing legal residence in the United States. Keep it in a safe place. Make a copy and send it along with the application. Also take the application for an invitation to your daughter, form number one hundred and thirty-one. Abigail and Sandra will help you fill it in...

"Well, that's all from us. Our mission is finished. We did everything we could. You have to sort out the rest of your immigration case. Remember, political asylum in America gives you many benefits, but there are also some disadvantages. You have to wait a very long time for a green card; I can't say how long you'll have to wait for citizenship. It will take many years. Perhaps in five years or even more, you get only a permanent-resident card. Then you have to wait another five years to get citizenship. But do not be discouraged. You have the same rights in America as all its citizens, except you can't vote and you can't be an employee of the government.

"My very important advice: avoid breaking the law, because in America they severely punish all those who break the law. This is especially true for immigrants. When they commit a crime, they are usually deported from the United States. Try to stay away from any conflict situations. Your main goal now is to find a job so you can independently support yourself and your daughter when she comes here. Your parents can come when you get citizenship and you are able to provide for them.

"Starting today you qualify for assistance from the government. For your information, there is a program of assistance to refugees. You will be given about five hundred dollars per month for six months. You will get a food card, which you can use to buy food at the supermarket in the amount of approximately three hundred dollars per month, and you can also have free medical services. There is a program under which you will be paid a housing benefit for your accommodation.

"You should contact social services. They will give you all the information there and you will get everything you are entitled to. We say good-bye to you—we have to go, because urgent cases are waiting for us—but your advocates will stay with you. We have finished our work. We wish you happiness. Good luck!" Dean Goldenberg and Professor Highland shook Slava's hand with a trace of sadness on their faces, and left in silence.

Slava felt sorry that she would probably never again see these people who were so dear to her, because she would be going her own way. She was in their company as equals. She knew that the highest happiness, reflecting the substance and the purpose of a person on Earth, was just to be a simple person among others for whom the highest value is a human life.

They understood each other without words, and were inspired by a great desire to win in the name of justice. They trusted each other, and it was natural and easy, without any special effort, the way it should be between people. Unfortunately, in her homeland she saw quite different relations between people, other values diametrically opposed to those she had seen and felt here in this overseas country, where hopes came true and there were great possibilities. This deeply wounded her soul. In a demoralized community of people, such phenomena as deception, betrayal, cynicism, and bribery become the norm. People do not want to seek the truth, which would liberate them; they are indifferent to themselves and to others, living in a degenerated society as paralyzed, deprived of the future. Slava had tried to help Ukrainian people by bringing the word of truth to them through her articles and books, but this true word hadn't come to their hearts. The teacher said the hopeless were those who didn't notice their slavery. To free a man like that was useless…

Slava was thinking about the fate of the people from which she had come. She put questions to herself many times: Why was this nation with deep historical roots, the offspring of legendary Aryans, Ants, Trypilians, Scythians, Rusychi, who gave the first human alphabet to the world, was the home of Vedic culture and a grain-producing civilization, with the highest fighting strength in the world (their knights had no equal)—today doomed to extinction? Why was the bridge between the descendants and the ancestors broken? The soul and the thoughts of the people who had secured the most beautiful and the richest space on planet Earth, the name of which is Ukraine now, had become smaller. They had abandoned their original spiritual values, the language of their native land was dying, they worshipped a strange faith, and they had lost the native Vedic culture their ancestors had been creating for thousands of years. Their instinct of self-defense was damaged, and the instinct of self-preservation was weak. They did not notice it themselves, that their national culture was slowly dissolving and being taken over by another nation, which sought to possess their ancient history and distinctive original culture. Why? These issues worried her constantly, and she and her colleagues discussed these subjects many times in the editor's office. They believed that the cause of all evils and misfortunes of Ukrainians lay in their centuries-old enslavement by the country's northern neighbor. Especially tragic for Ukrainians was the Soviet period when Communism was built and artificially created a new community of Soviet people without any signs of nationality and with an atheistic world outlook. Happy were those people who did not know what it meant to live under Communism, who hadn't become victims of this hideous experiment of the twentieth century, as had happened with the Ukrainians.

The same day of the court hearing Slava called the teacher. He was very happy to hear the news that the judge had granted her political asylum, and warmly congratulated her on the successful completion of the immigration proceedings.

American Dream

It is natural that man is constantly in search of something new and unexplored. This is the only way to gain experience. And although the experience of mankind has accumulated over thousands of years, there still exists unachievable knowledge that was owned by our ancestors. A person in this world is limited in his ability to fulfill himself. It seems that this world is not open enough for humans. It is tight. Somewhere there is a more perfect world, where a person can express himself, where nothing restricts him in his spiritual development. It seemed that America had created the most advanced civilization on the planet, aimed at the material welfare of people, and for this purpose there is a certain stereotype, a perfect model to inspire people: the American dream. It is based on the fact that only by honest, hard work can you achieve all the things that make you happy. Does a person come into this world for material values? Slava thought about this many times, and the experience of her life in America showed that it's human nature to find self-satisfaction in trials. The person in this life achieves what he seeks, and finds himself in the place that he chooses. There is a causal-consequence law of nature, and no one manages to escape from it. Everyone is the creator of their destiny. The teacher said this to her, and she was convinced of it after passing her tests and gaining her experience in this life.

Two years had passed since Slava was granted the status of a political asylum in America. She lived in Washington, DC, in front of the famous Watergate building and the big concert hall, the Kennedy Center. For two years she worked in the Institute of Diplomatic Service of the US State Department, where she taught the Ukrainian language. She liked this job; she taught the American diplomats who had been appointed to work with the US embassy in Ukraine. Among the students was also the US ambassador to Ukraine. The American diplomats admired their teacher; they liked her method of teaching: the lessons were unconventional. She used "live" teaching methods, which included direct communication with each student. They talked freely in the classroom with the teacher on any subject, laughed, joked, and even cried, looking at true tragic stories about the famine and about the Chernobyl disaster. They were not given much time to learn a foreign language—from six to eight months, depending on the rank of the diplomat. And during that time they had to learn enough words to communicate in everyday language for the so-called survival course. Together with their teacher, they celebrated their birthdays and arranged Ukrainian parties, where they prepared Ukrainian food— varenyky (pierogi, dumplings), piroshki (stuffed buns), blinchiky (pancakes), and borsch (kind of vegetable soup)—and listened to Ukrainian music. They visited different shows and folklore festivals organized by Ukrainians in Baltimore and Silver Spring (Maryland), and even traveled to New York for Easter.

When diplomats went to Ukraine, their first wish was to visit Slava's family. Slava's dad and mum always welcomed guests from America: her mother treated them to delicious Ukrainian food, and her father told them of Ukrainian customs and traditions. He introduced them to Ukrainian poetry and folklore, and taught them to sing melodious Ukrainian songs together. When the ambassador arrived in Ukraine, he invited Slava's father, mother, and daughter to the US embassy; he was interested in meeting her family. He talked freely with them in Ukrainian, and said that he had learned it so well thanks to his teacher Slava. Her parents were proud for their daughter. Subsequently, an article appeared in the newspaper *Svoboda* (New Jersey, 2001), under the heading "Ukrainian Teacher of the American Ambassador." In this publication the US ambassador to Ukraine thanked his teacher for her professionalism, her desire to make lessons interesting, her lucidity, and her comprehensive introduction of the culture and traditions of Ukrainian people and its history; he stated, "She brought the charms of the Ukrainian people to my heart that helped me get to know the country where I will work."

As the result of the proposal by the ambassador and the financial support of the US-Ukraine Foundation at the George Washington University, for the first time in the history of the university, Ukrainian section in the Department of German and Slavic Languages and Literatures was opened. Slava was invited to chair this newly created section. In fact, it was part of the project by the Elliott Institute of

International Affairs at the George Washington University. Slava planned and developed the course on Ukrainian language, culture, and history over two semesters, and wrote a textbook for university students. She received a grant of $1,500 for her work from the Elliott Institute, and $2,000 from the Ukrainian Credit Union in Chicago to write a textbook on Ukrainian language. The cultural and educational foundation in California, named after Halia Shcherban-Lapika , created by Ray Lapika in honor of his wife, awarded Slava a prize of $5,000 for originality, uniqueness, and a new vision of the history, language, and culture without Soviet stereotypes and foreign influences in her publications. In her book Slava wrote that the language must be not only learned but felt: the natural sound of language we can find in myths, poetry, folksongs, ballads, parables, legends, and fairy tales. She stated that Ukrainian language belongs to the original languages; probably, it is the oldest language on the planet Earth, and its root can be traced deep into the ages of 40,000 years. It was spoken by the creators of ancient Trypilian culture and civilization. Proof of this Slava found in authoritative sources of Western linguists. For example, scientist A. Diamont in the book *The History and Origin of Language* (1959) wrote, that in the steppes of Eastern Europe (on present-day Ukrainian territory) more than 5,000 years ago the Indo-European language appeared, its dialects divided into languages which extended many nations. And this is not a discovery: the British Library and the Library of Mexico City University— on the wall have a map of movements of Aryan tribes about 6,000 years ago who came from the steppe regions and north-western shores of the Black Sea to the west and the south. Thus, ancient history begins not in Sumer (historical region in southern Mesopotamia, modern Iraq), not in Babylon, but in the territory of ancient Ukraine. This is confirmed by recent findings of archaeologists.

Slava advised students to borrow from the Library of Congress (Washington DC) the book *The story of English* (by Robert McCrum, William Cran, Robert MacNeil, 1986), where they can read the above statements themselves and see map of movements of ancient tribes.

To make it interesting for the students to study Ukrainian language, Slava included, for example, some words that Ukrainian ancestors spoke, taken from Sanskrit, then modern Ukrainian, and English translation: *tata, tato [father]; tapa, teplo [heat]; dyv, dyvo [wonder]; nana, nenya [mother]; tana, tonka [thin]; agni, vohon [fire], svastya, shchastya [fortune, good luck]; dasan, desyat' [ten]; dva, dva [two]; Veda, Bedy [Vedas, knowledge]; vidata, vidaty [to know]; piti, pyty [to drink]; dati, daty [to give]; nava, nova [new]; ida, yida [food]; dara, doroha [dear]; ati, ity [to go]; plava, plavaty [to swim]; bhuta, buty [to be]; lada, ladna [pretty]; tata, tato [father]; vesanta, vesna [spring]* plus many-many other words that she took from the *Comparative Sanskrit-English-Ukrainian Dictionary*, which was made by the teacher while he was in India. This was the first such dictionary in comparative linguistics in the Ukrainian language. All started from it; later on, linguists in Ukraine referred to it, adding and expanding, and actually coming to the same conclusion made by the teacher: Sanskrit is the closest to the modern Ukrainian language. This is the most convincing evidence that the oldest language came is the mother of the Indo-European languages.

Slava told her students, "The author of this comparative dictionary, Dr. Lev Sylenko, affirms that in Sanskrit are also the words which today are used in the homes of the Ukrainian villages, and these words cannot be found in the Ukrainian dictionaries because they are forbidden by censorship. It is marvelous that the words that lived in the villages of Trypillia (Tripolye) 7,000 years ago are still living in Sanskrit and in the homes of Ukrainian villages today.

"The eminent American historian and philosopher Will Durant in his 11 volumes "The Story of Civilization" (1935 – 1975) wrote: "Sanskrit - the mother of European languages… Sanskrit is the most ancient and perfect among the languages of the world."

Slava told her student about scholarly contributions of Sir William Jones (1746 -1794), Anglo-Welsh philologist and researcher of ancient India. She said:

"Of all his discoveries, William Jones is known today for making and propagation the observation that classical Greek and Latin had been derived from Sanskrit. In his Third Anniversary Discourse to the Asiatic Society (1786) he suggested that classical Greek and Latin had a common root – Sanskrit – and that the two may be further related, in turn, to Gothic and the Celtic languages, as well as to Persian. Sir William Jones uttered the following memorable words, which have often been quoted as the beginning of comparative linguistics and Indo-European studies and in books on the history of linguistics:

"The Sanskrit language, whatever be its antiquity, is of a wonderful structure; more perfect than the Greek, more copious than the Latin, and more exquisitely refined than either, yet bearing to both of them a stronger affinity, both in the roots of verbs and the forms of grammar, than could possibly have been produced by accident; so strong indeed, that no philologer could examine them all three, without believing them to have sprung from some common source, which, perhaps, no longer exists; there is a similar reason, though not quite so forcible, for supposing that both the Gothic and the Celtic, though blended with a very different idiom, had the same origin with the Sanskrit; and the old Persian might added to the same family." (Otto Jespersen, "Language: Its Nature, Development and Origin", 1964) This common source came to be known as Proto-Indo-European. Jones was the first to propose a racial division of India involving an Aryan invasion but at that time there was insufficient evidence to support it.

"The famous English writer Herbert G. Wells in his bestselling three-volume work, "The Outline of History" (1920) wrote: "But even this original Aryan language [Sanskrit] , which was a spoken speech perhaps 6,000 or 5,000 B.C., was by no means a primordial language… Its earliest speakers were at or past the Neolithic stage of civilization. It had grammatical forms and verbal devices of some complexity. The vanished methods of expression of the later Paleolithic peoples, of the Azilians, or of the early Neolithic kitchen-midden people for instance, were probably cruder than the most elementary form of Aryan… Probably the Aryan group of languages became distinct in a wide region of which the Danube, Dnieper, Don." (P.118-119).

During her classes Slava had introduced a variety of teaching materials, most of which she had developed on her own; she made a point of introducing different aspects of Ukrainian language, history and culture. By offering these materials and explaining their significance, she helped students develop a better intuitive feel for customs and practices that are important to the Ukrainian people.

Once, the American ambassador asked the professor, if the Ukrainian language is derived from the Russian or is a Russian dialect. Slava answered, "Sadly—but it is a fact—today in the West, many dictionaries and textbooks contain information written back in the Soviet time by the supporters of Soviet ideological language doctrine that justified the colonial expansion of the empire of the USSR. It contradicts the true history, and took away the sacred right of every nation to speak its native language in the name of "one and indivisible" and "a great and powerful" Russian language. It took the northern neighbor three centuries of enslavement of the Ukrainian people and a lot of effort to destroy the Ukrainian language and even prohibit it. This stereotype of humiliation and contempt for the Ukrainian language, unfortunately, exists in Moscow today, despite the fact that the independent state – Ukraine - appeared on the map of Europe in 1991. If there is such a country, it means the language is alive. But the history and the origin of the Ukrainian language still are little known in the world. This situation must be corrected now, first of all to provide the truth about the Ukrainian language and its history—not on racial, national, or religious grounds, but in the name of justice. Among the nations was agreement, mutual respect, and peace in the name of holy wisdom and truth, and as brothers, we have to recognize each other. These concepts are sacred and very dear to every nation.

"Facts and only the true facts can discredit the Moscow stereotypes that were created over the centuries about the Ukrainians and their language. The truth of history's science proves that the original language of Kievan Rus that is an old Ukrainian already existed. Kievan Rus was at that time a strong Kingdom, and the language of the Moscow Principality began to emerge only in the 11th century. Before that time Moscow was never mentioned; it just did not exist. According to Hypation chronicle, Moscow was mentioned for the first time in these words: "Prince Yuri Dolhoruky gave a great dinner in 1147 in Moscow" (considered to be the official age of Moscow), and the Russian historian Nikolay Karamzin wrote about it in *History of the Russian State (a 12-volume history)* where it is also mentioned that Kievan Prince Yuri Dolgorukiy (literally "Yuri the Long Armed"), the son of the Grand Prince of Kievan Rus Volodymyr Monomakh, in 1121-1157 invaded the lands that were inhabited by local tribes of Ugro-Finns, and these lands were called the Great Principality of Moscow. (At that time, such names as "Russia" did not exist.) Kniaz (Prince) Yuri Dolgorukiy was a founder of Moscow and Vladimir-Suzdal Grand Dukes. However, today the antique prints and chronicles no longer exist; they were burned on the orders of the Moscow rulers. Nikolay Karamzin in his *History of the Russian State* proved that Moscow state was formed by aristocrats of the Golden Horde, Mongol Khanate (during the invasion of Khan Baty) who became relatives with the daughters and sons of the princes of Kiev, Novgorod, Suzdal, and others. They adopted Greek Orthodox religion and became the builders of the Moscow empire that was named Russia by the tsar Peter the First, from the word *Rus'* (Kievan Rus)."

Slava organized a presentation of her textbook in the Department of German and Slavic Languages and Literatures at her university. After the presentation, which was also attended by professors from other universities, she was asked to read the lectures in Ukrainian studies for one semester at Georgetown University. Of course, she agreed, because this university had opened the way to the American dream for her, and from here she had begun her journey into American life…

She also worked as a special adviser to the State Department, was a language instructor at the International Center for Language Studies and the Defense Language Institute, and taught evening courses at the Department of Justice. Slava used a comprehensive language teaching method that including listening comprehension, speaking, reading and writing during the 90-minute sessions. She worked very intensively with the students and they were very pleased with her teaching. Slava received many offers from various government institutions and private schools, but had chosen only those closest to her place of residence on 2450 Virginia Avenue near the Watergate. The day was too short to work in several institutions at the same time; there were periods when she had ten lessons a day. Her working day began at seven o'clock in the morning and ended at nine o'clock. In the summer time she didn't refuse to go to Texas for two months to teach the Russian language to American pilots. A high-ranking military pilot-astronaut from the space agency NASA asked her if she had ever dreamed, as a young girl in school in Ukraine, that one day she would be a professor for the officer-pilots at the US Air Force Academy. Slava was touched by these words of an American man. She barely hid her excitement and said she had never thought about it. She thanked him for his kind words toward her and said she was one of those lucky people who were lucky to be here when they needed her among those people whose dreams came true too... the American dream.

Slava got to work with the American elite; she was delighted by these wonderful people. These were people with a well-developed sense of dignity, who knew their duty as citizens and fulfilled their obligation in good and honest ways. These people were open, not pinned down by any ideological, political, or religious frames. These people were free; it was easy to communicate with them. In Ukraine, with the exception of her parents and a few of the older generation of intellectuals, she had never met such people. The slavery for many centuries—the Communist system—had left its mark on the Ukrainian people. Wherever you went in Ukraine, you could witness blackmail, treachery, deceit, and bribery; corruption was at every step. It is difficult to cure people from having been slaves for centuries. The Ukrainian man who traveled in the West and directly faced the life of the highly developed countries of Europe or America, whether working or studying, and then returned home, found it almost impossible to adapt to the terrible Ukrainian routine.

He didn't have something he had while he was there: the right of choice, the right to be a free person. For this taste of freedom a person may give everything, even his life.

In several years Slava had reached success in her career in America. She was convinced that in America a person has all the possibilities to realize their abilities. This required only a great desire and the willpower to be a decent person and to be a professional in your work; everything else came as a heavy rain on a sunny summer day. In the country where she was born, it was not possible to achieve the same way it was in America.

Finally Slava received a letter from US Immigration Services that said her daughter was invited to an interview with the US embassy in Moscow. At that time the US embassy in Kiev did not issue immigrant visas for permanent residence (indefinite leave to remain in the USA). A month after receiving this letter, her daughter went with her mother Maria, Lelya's grandmother, to Moscow for an interview. Permission to travel to the United States was successfully obtained; Lelya had gotten a visa. But she had had to wait for more than two years. The thing that most worried Slava was her daughter's visit. She wanted it to happen soon, because it was dangerous for the whole family to stay in Ukraine, and she was worried about her daughter.

It was the summer holidays' time. Classes at the university had ended, and her new contract began on the first of September. Slava went to Spring Glen to visit the teacher and stayed there during vacations. She had visited the teacher before, mainly on holidays and weekends. He felt very lonely; he rented a small house in the mountains, where he spent his days in meditation and in his thoughts. Most Ukrainians who came to the temple did not understand the teacher; they could not understand his spiritual science. They were more interested not in spirituality but in the wealth of this world. The teacher saw it, and couldn't be surrounded by such people. He was a highly spiritual, enlightened man, which is why he lived alone among the magic of nature in the mountains. His eyesight had deteriorated more; he was an elderly man and didn't drive. Slava used his car. She brought him enough food for several weeks. She was the only person he trusted and welcomed into its cozy, modest home, which consisted of two rooms: a living room and a small kitchen. Slava helped him reply to the letters that he received from around the world, sorted out his domestic affairs, and did the cooking. But what she liked the most was to sit during the warm summer evenings on the wooden deck, look at the stars in sky, and listen to the stories of the teacher about the life of the ancestors, about where life had come to the land, and the possible existence of life on other planets. He opened many mysteries of this world to her, and passed to her his prediction that awaits humanity in the future. She kept every word of the teacher in her heart, and as the time came, she would tell what the teacher predicted.

One August evening, the teacher was not as calm as usual. Something was worrying him, but he did not tell Slava what it was. The very next day Slava was going to go to Kennedy Airport in New York to meet her daughter. When she came out of the house in the morning with the teacher, there was a bird near the doorstep that had banged against the door and didn't show signs of life. The teacher walked Slava to the bus stop but never told her why he was so upset. This anxiety was passed to Slava. Her soul was troubled, she felt something was wrong, and the strange feeling stayed with her all day. She did not understand what was going on with her.

Her daughter's flight was expected at nine o'clock. In her heart she was worried. Slava was praying that nothing had happened to her daughter. The long-awaited moment came. The plane arrived late. Slava had stood about two hours at the section marked "Arrivals" and looked into the distance, where many people had passed through passport control. Lelya was not there. Almost all the passengers who arrived from Warsaw had left passport control. Slava began to worry. But suddenly in the distance appeared a slim girl with a blond plait who went confidently to the door, pulling a suitcase on wheels behind her. The corridor was long enough that Slava could run to meet her, but the airport staff stopped her. Then Slava shouted her daughter's name, and she heard her and sped up her steps. Finally they hugged each other. Slava held her daughter to herself firmly and didn't release her: they both cried for joy. It was the happiest moment in their lives because they hadn't seen each other for nine long years. They were finally together after a long separation. Her daughter saw the bright lights of New York at night for the first time, on their way from Kennedy Airport to Spring Glen.

That memorable evening they had tea with sweets together and went to bed after a short conversation. Lelya was very happy to see her mother after all those years of separation. She was tired after a sixteen-hour flight with a transfer in Warsaw, so they decided to talk the next day. Slava was very excited about meeting her daughter; she was immensely happy that they were finally together. The teacher was also glad that the daughter was with her mother, and that they had happily reached Spring Glen. The anxiety on his face disappeared as soon as he saw Slava with her daughter. He had turned on the lights everywhere and sat in the yard, even though it was a late hour, waiting for them to arrive from the airport.

Before going to sleep, the teacher told Slava to call her parents and comfort them, because they cared about Lelya. Slava called her mother in Kiev to say that everything was good, that Lelya had had a long flight, landed safely, and was doing well. Mum said that she did not sleep all night and was waiting for her call; it was eight o'clock in the morning in Kiev. Her mother's voice sounded tired, but she as always was gentle and careful. Mum said that Slava had to do everything possible for Lelya to continue her study at the university, because she was a talented child and should learn. And her last words were, "I did everything possible for your daughter to be with you. Stay together always, and I'll stay beside you there… I'm happy now. Now I am going to work."

Slava went to bed and felt that she was in a strange state. She had a headache and her legs didn't listen to her; it was difficult for her to make any moves. She thought it was because of the previous day's excitement and fatigue, and reassured herself that it would soon go away…

In the morning Slava proposed to Lelya that they can go to nearby town Kingston. Lelya agreed.

Behind the wheel of her Lincoln, Slava still didn't feel well, although she was able to drive. Her daughter carefully observed all around; it was her first day in America. She was interested in everything around her. First they went to the supermarket and bought just enough food for dinner. Then they went to the big mall, where Lelya chose clothes and shoes for every day. When they returned home, they prepared dinner.

Slava took a roasted turkey from the oven and had just laid it on the table to serve when the phone rang. She picked up the phone. She heard heavy breathing and then a sudden sobbing of her brother, who forced himself to say, "Mother was killed... car... she was taken to the morgue. Father is there. It is very bad for him..." Slava did not hear any more of her brother's words. She lost consciousness. When she came around, she realized what was going on. Lelya and the teacher were next to her. They learned from her brother what had happened. Slava's mother went to the hospital for her daily job in the morning; she was a pedestrian and got hit by the car. The teacher wiped the tears on his face, and for a moment he covered his face with his hands and bowed his head. Her daughter was frightened and pale. Only yesterday her grandmother had seen her off..., her beloved and dear grandmother.... Yesterday morning she had been taken to the airport by her most dear grandmother and grandfather... And suddenly there was no close and dear person.

At the moment it seemed that they simply could not accept what had happened, the idea that Slava's mother was taken from her life, was no longer alive, and had left her dearest family and relatives and gone into another world. They were all like one family feeling an unbearable soul ache. To Slava it seemed that with the loss of her mother, she lost herself. For the next months she was in this terrible condition... She could not come to terms with what happened...

The American ambassador wrote a letter to Slava, "I was terribly saddened to learn of your mother's death. I'm sure it had to be all the more difficult to bear given your separation over the past years. We will keep her and your family in our thoughts and prayers."

Her political emigrant status did not let Slava go to Ukraine to say farewell to her mother's body. This caused her severe pain. When she called US Immigration Services to get permission to go to her mother's funeral, she was refused. She was not allowed to go to her native country where she was born... The killing of people in Ukraine there had become the norm... In that country the life of a man was worthless... Oh, God, what despair and pain, what great disappointment Slava experienced after the death of her mother...

When Slava's father submitted a statement to the prosecution to bring the driver of the Mercedes to responsibility for the murder of his wife, they began to follow him and intimidate him. Near the door of his flat some young people were on duty late at night several times; they banged the door and shouted in Russian, "Open up. We have come to talk to you. Take your statement from the prosecutor's office; our boss did not kill her..." Her father tried to protect himself and phoned the police, but the police did not come, saying there was no one to send, that a district police officer was on call on another case. Then he asked his friends to come, but by the time they came, the young skinheads had disappeared. So her father was terrorized for a month, until he stopped going to the prosecutor. In one of his visits, the investigator who was dealing with her mother's murder went with her father out on the street and said, "I would advise you not to come here anymore, because the case with your wife could be repeated. As you know, you are dealing with the mafia. The market director is in charge of it, of who killed your wife. Think about yourself."

After that, her father did not see this investigator. He was told that the investigator was on a long-term mission.

At the first trial, which her father attended, despite the threats, he was shocked by the falsification of facts. Even the name of the accused wasn't the one he had seen in the original records of the investigation, in the notes taken on the day of the tragic murder. The father's heart could not stand it. He ended up in the hospital. On the phone to Slava he said that he would not go over there again, that he just would not survive the abuse and cynicism... And he did not go over there. They stopped watching him, and the threats disappeared. The court's decision was in favor of the accused, who was a substitute; they just closed the case in the absence of any evidence of a crime. However, the court's decision was not sent to Slava's father. About a year later her father accidentally bumped into the investigator on Khreshchatyk (the central street in Kiev) who advised him not to go to the court and mysteriously disappeared without bringing the matter to the end. He told her father that the case was closed for lack of evidence of a crime, that all the facts were made up, as well as the expertise, and there was a substitute in the case. He said he knew who the killer was, but that he (the investigator) had been suspended from the matter. He had moved to another job and had nothing to do with this case. He said there was already bribery, and that the judge who conducted the case had received a promotion. He also said that starting to fight with the mafia was useless in that country; you had to go abroad, take the matter to foreign lawyers, and start all over again...

Her father was not going to leave Ukraine. He said that he was born there, spent his best years with his dearest wife there, and would live out his years there, closer to her... But the pain in his heart for the loss of the person closest to him would remain forever.

There was no justice in Ukraine; you could not find it there.

Slava was thinking, *Why in Ukraine is there a deformed human consciousness and why have people lost their human virtues, without which men cannot live? The double oppression influenced the consciousness of the Ukrainians: forced to take someone else's faith 1,000 years ago; Moscovite oppression of Ukrainians that lasted more than 300 years; a ban on the Ukrainian language, culture, and history; persecution of the noble Ukrainian people; Stalin's repressions, the Holodomor, Chernobyl disaster... Is there a nation with as tragic a history as Ukraine? We still feel the effects of deformation and destruction of the soul consciousness of Ukrainian people...*

The past should be remembered so that we can move forward, and we descendants must heal the wound of our predecessors. Worthy is one who can correct the mistakes of ancestors. Someone made a mistake by implementing the aliens' faith in Ukraine. Already more than 1,000 years passed since the irreparable disaster happened. But we still feel the effects of deformation and destruction of the soul consciousness of Ukrainian people.

The talent of Ukrainian people and their spiritual greatness is judged on the basis of the values of their unique world view and the spirituality that is their alone, that came from their ancestors and had its roots in the Trypilian culture, as described in man's oldest spiritual books, the Vedas. The true knowledge about the Universe, human beings and the past of Mankind was hiding for centuries. If a person does not know who he is, what he is capable of, and what he was born for, he can easily become a slave. This idea laid in the foundation of modern civilization…But, in fact, every person is born for a purpose. We are all part of the Whole, cells of the vast Universe, the great Creature, whom people call – God. And each of us has the potential of the Universe itself, God himself. We just need to wake up and realize who we are, what we live for and how these possibilities can be discovered inside ourselves. Today we need action. The people need spiritual education, and they need the truth. And when they know the truth, they shall be set free. The wisdom of our ancestors tells us:

Rich is one, who with avarice does not impoverish himself;

Happy is the one who wishes happiness for people;

Glorified is the one, who glorifies himself with his valorous work;

Noble is the one, who suffers for the truth and awaits compassion from no one;

Truthful is the one, who glorifies a truthful man;

Beautiful is the one, who has a beautiful soul;

Courageous is the one, whom loneliness does not frighten;

Smart is the one, who respects wisdom, which is beneficial for his nation;

Educated is the one, who knows how to enrich himself with the true knowledge;

Talented is the one, who is able to devote his talents to the people;

Do not rejoice when you see that your joy grieves others;

Do not ease life for yourself by burdening the life of people;

Live with the willingness to be a better person tomorrow than you are today;

Live in order that your life has many joys which you share with others, and then others will share your grief with you;

Man is the child of Heaven and Earth. On the planet Earth there is nothing more beautiful than a man. Love is freedom. Love is the brightest feeling that is in man – love to beauty, love to knowledge and love to Mother Nature. Man must love himself honestly; the one who does not love himself, cannot love another. Without love a man cannot be a man. Love helps man to look with inspiration on life and the world. Love is the manifestation of independence of the human. A man in love strives to improve himself, to better understand himself, the people and the world. Love is the prayer of the soul, the great treasure of Heaven and Earth… Live in love, help each other, explore the world and your spirit will be strong forever!

Slava kept in her memory every tragic and fortunate moment in her life. She never forgot how she was granted asylum in America. This process had taken a very long time, but she had gone through this interesting and very stressful period in her life and gotten a real experience of American democracy. She got the most precious gift in this world: freedom. That gift didn't have a price.

Her daughter successfully graduated with honors from the George Washington University, one of the top five students of her class. When she appeared on the stage to make a speech, the president of the university started to read the essay she had written for admission to the university four years earlier:

"Approximately 33,000 feet above the Earth, I couldn't shake the feeling that something was terribly wrong. However, it wasn't until six hours later, with my feet firmly planted on the ground, that my mother delivered the shocking news. As I was on my way to America, my grandmother had been brutally killed in what police described as a 'suspicious accident.'

"My mother is a journalist who fled Ukraine because she was persecuted for her democratic and anti-totalitarian beliefs. Her life was threatened, and she was granted political asylum in the United States. During that time, I lived with my grandparents and we also had to endure death threats and were even violently attacked several times. On one such occasion, as I nursed my grandmother's wounds, I never lost sight of my dreams or my goals.

"Growing up in Ukraine, I knew exactly who I was. Star athlete (track and field), straight A student, devoted granddaughter, and trusted friend. I studied like there was no tomorrow and strove for perfection in anything I touched. Whether it was dance, theater, or writing for my college newspaper, my end goal was always the same: to earn a PhD in biochemistry. I won the Best Science Report award for my research into the effects of Chernobyl on living organisms. I also took part in the academic Olympiad in biology, mathematics, chemistry, English, and Ukrainian languages and received numerous awards. There was nothing that stood in my way.

"But my grandmother's death changed all that. I began to question my choices and wondered if my drive and ambition were a waste. After all, if human life is worth so little, why strive for anything? I found myself losing interest in what used to excite me.

"But then one day, as I was strolling through the streets of my new homeland, I saw a little flower peering through the thick snow that was spread on the field like white frosting. Stopping along the road, I leaned over and tried to figure out how the little flower could not only survive, but also obviously thrive under such harsh conditions. Although it looked very fragile, it was obviously also very strong. And as I was inspecting that little purple flower, I saw my drive and determination gathered on the purple petals. My grandmother nurtured those same qualities in me, and not even the worst conditions could kill the seedling she planted inside me.

"There are good days and there are not-so-good days, but even during some dark hours, I still know what I want, and I'm not afraid to work hard to achieve it. I want to study and I need to learn. After all, now I have someone watching over me. And I cannot disappoint her, because that would mean her death was in vain. But I know deep in my heart that it wasn't…"

Slava was crying from happiness, she was proud of her daughter. At that moment Slava felt the presence of her mother. She realized that her mother lived in her heart, in the heart of her daughter, and even death could not kill the seedlings her mother planted inside her and her daughter; she was watching over her and her granddaughter…

Lelya was admitted to a PhD program in biochemistry at Harvard University after graduating from the George Washington University. In five years she graduated with a PhD diploma and became a rising star scientist in the fields of biochemistry and immunology.

After many years of teaching Slava became one of the most respected spiritual teachers and authors. Having experienced both success and failure in her life, she was poised at last on the brink of her greatest fulfillment: a life of mastery and understanding that provided not only her, but the entire world. Slava knew deep in her heart what it was meant to be lived and to be free in this world...